The Development of Socialist Economic Thought

The Development of Socialist Economic Thought

Selected Essays by Maurice Dobb

Edited and introduced by
Brian Pollitt

AAKAR

THE DEVELOPMENT OF SOCIALIST ECONOMIC THOUGHT
Edited and introduced by Brian Pollitt

First Published in India 2014

ISBN 978-93-5002-253-5

Published in agreement with Lawrence and Wishart Limited, London for publication and sale only in the Indian Subcontinent (India, Pakistan, Bangladesh, Nepal, Maldives, Bhutan and Sri Lanka)

Published by
AAKAR BOOKS
28 E Pocket IV, Mayur Vihar Phase I, Delhi 110 091
Phone : 011 2279 5505 Telefax : 011 2279 5641
info@aakarbooks.com; www.aakarbooks.com

Printed at
Mudrak, 30 A Patparganj, Delhi 110 091

Contents

Preface

Maurice Dobb was the foremost and most versatile scholar of his day in Marxian political economy and areas of economic history. On his death in 1976 he left a wealth of manuscripts and printed versions of lectures, articles and books written since 1920. There was also correspondence received from friends and associates, mostly dating from 1948. As his Literary Executor, I assembled and gave preliminary order to this material while visiting Trinity College, Cambridge in 1983-84. On the death in 1984 of his wife, Barbara, most of the material was gifted to the College and, over the following years, an archive of Dobb Papers was formally established there in the Wren Library. While Dobb's letters to others were hand-written and he made no copies, many became available when gifted to the archive by a number of their recipients or when located in diverse collections of Papers established for distinguished scholars elsewhere.

On his death Dobb left no major unpublished works or significant works-in-progress. Immediately before and after his retirement in 1967, however, he submitted a number of essays to various encyclopaedias, some of which were published in English and some in translation. He also delivered a number of unpublished lectures and contributed to publications – such as the *Annali* of the Istituto Giangiacomo Feltrinelli and the journal *Socialist Europe* – that proved short-lived and/or of very limited accessibility. From such sources, it was possible to bring together a selection of his lesser-known essays on socialist economic thought and planning which, since not overly technical in nature, was also appropriate for the non-specialist reader.

While assembling Dobb's papers, I benefited greatly from the selfless collaboration of Professor Bruce McFarlane, who, over several years, worked with me in, especially, Trinity College, Cambridge and at the Universities of Adelaide and Glasgow. My debt to him is very great.

I must also thank Sally Davison of Lawrence & Wishart for editorial assistance made the more taxing by the varied formats in which the typescripts and printed versions of Dobb's essays were initially presented. Errors of interpretation, of course, are all mine.

Brian H. Pollitt

Acknowledgements

'Socialist thought' was originally an entry for the *International Encyclopedia of Social Sciences*, Vol. 4, edited by D.L. Sills and published by Macmillan New York. It was written in 1966 and published in 1968.

'The centenary of *Capital* and its relevance today' was originally a lecture to the Marx Memorial Library, 17 March 1967, to mark the centenary of the publication of Volume I of *Capital.*

'The Discussions of the 1920s about Building Socialism' was written in 1964 for the *Annali* of the Istituto Feltrinelli of Milan. Feltrinelli eventually published it in English in 1967.

'Planning' is published here in the original English version. It was written in 1972 and published only in translation in the *Enciclopedia Italiana* (Garzanti 1976).

'Commodity-Production under Socialism' was originally read to a seminar organised by the Committee for the Study of European Socialist Countries at Cambridge in May 1976. It was transcribed from his manuscript notes and published posthumously, later in 1976, in the short-lived journal *Socialist Europe.*

Introduction

Most academic accounts of the history of economic thought neglect the body of literature concerned with the development of planned socialist economies. There is no valid reason for this, since some path-breaking modern contributions to 'western' models of growth and development trod ground that had already been mapped by Soviet economists concerned to identify the building blocks of growth and planning in the USSR of the 1920s. Moreover, the subsequent process of Soviet development held great interest for many newly independent countries after World War II, their efforts to develop industry and create wealth for their newly liberated peoples encountering many of the obstacles previously confronted by Soviet planners.

For more than fifty years, Maurice Dobb reflected on the issues faced by those seeking to promote growth in non-industrialised countries. He was also concerned to establish Marx's rightful place in the history of political economy. For Dobb, Marxian political economy developed logically from the work of the classical economists – most notably Ricardo – and he opposed the views of later economists who rejected or (like Keynes) ignored the theories advanced in *Das Kapital*. Dobb further stressed that the more creative writings on the political economy of socialism are demonstrably rooted not only in Marx but also, through him, in the classical tradition as a whole.

The selection of Dobb's writings on socialist economic thought and planning brought together on this book represent his later thinking on the subject. This included critical appraisals of aspects of Soviet policy and performance – which, it must be said, have been ignored by a number of writers who have portrayed him as a life-long apologist for Soviet-style socialism; his critique, of course, was to be more than justified by later developments. In their totality, however, his essays give greater substance to a model of development based on socialism rather than capitalism.

This sample of Dobb's later work on a particular theme is, of course, best appreciated when located within his more general contributions to political economy and economic history. Before going on to introduce the particular essays collected in this volume, we therefore offer a brief outline of Dobb's life and work.

DOBB'S ECONOMIC WRITINGS

1924-1950

Maurice Dobb was born in London in 1900. Educated at Charterhouse School and at Pembroke College, Cambridge, he completed his PhD at the London School of Economics. On taking up a post as Lecturer in economics at Cambridge in 1924, he published his doctoral research as *Capitalist Enterprise and Social Progress* (Dobb, 1925). He was later to describe this work as 'an unsuccessful and jejune attempt to combine the notion of surplus-value and exploitation with the theory of Marshall' (Dobb, 1978, p117), but the product of his researches into the history of capitalism proved more valuable when later deployed in his path-breaking *Studies in the Development of Capitalism* (Dobb, 1946).

Dobb joined the British Communist Party in 1922, and in 1925 travelled to live and work in Moscow. His first-hand observations there gave him unusual insight into the emergence of the Soviet economy over its first stormy decade. His major work on *Russian Economic Development since the Revolution* (Dobb, 1928A) made him known to a wide international audience. This was partly because of the compelling, if mostly hostile, interest aroused worldwide by the Bolshevik revolution but also because Dobb's account was the first detailed analysis by a professional economist of the evolution of Soviet economic debate and strategy prior to the implementation of the first five-year plan in 1929. Maynard Keynes, who had also visited Moscow in 1925 and whose exchanges with Soviet planners were witnessed by Dobb, read and generally approved Dobb's work, which was reviewed – for the most part respectfully – in newspapers and journals as far afield as the United States, Shanghai, Tokyo and Australia. The second edition, also published in 1928, concluded with an uncommonly timely Appendix 'On Agriculture and Industry in 1927-28' (ibid, pp409-30), in which Dobb reviewed the principal contending schools of thought on the most desirable future course for Soviet development and planning. This remarkable discussion – ended by Stalin mere months after Dobb had here summarised it – embraced cardinal developmental issues that failed to be addressed by non-Marxian economists in the West until the 1950s and 1960s, when the need to counter planning models inspired by Soviet experience focused greater attention on the development problems of the Third World. Dobb himself was later able to draw extensively on his 1928 volume when it was updated in both 1948 and 1966 as *Soviet Economic Development since 1917* (Dobb, 1948 and 1966).

In 1928, Dobb also authored the Cambridge Economic Handbook on *Wages* (Dobb, 1928B). Commissioned by Keynes and Dennis Robertson, this work was a physically trim but intellectually substantial contribution to institutional economics, and the editors' choice of Dobb to write it reflected their confidence in his ability to produce an accessible but rigorous review of the theory and practice of wage-determination. It also reflected the fact that there were few other academic economists of the day who could be counted on to have sufficient knowledge of or interest in the institutions of both labour and capital. Keynes, for one, reported Dobb to be an able critic of the prevailing orthodoxies of the theory of distribution, and generally approved of his emphasis on the potential of politics and bargaining power to influence wage-levels (Keynes, 1930, p114).

In 1932, Dobb made his first significant appraisal of the history of economic thought in his slender *An Introduction to Economics* (Dobb, 1932). While he was to treat the development of economic thought from the classical economists to contemporary theorists at much greater length in later years, this early work was of interest not least because it revealed the first explicit influence on his thinking of the Italian economist Piero Sraffa (ibid, p35, footnote 1). As will shortly be shown, this relationship – begun in 1922 and ended only with Dobb's death in 1976 – was to be of great significance for both men in the 1950s and 1960s. While the 1932 text had a limited academic impact at the time – it was written for a lay, not a professional, audience – its translated version serves to this day as a lucid introduction to economics for students in Mexico and elsewhere in Latin America.

While Dobb continued, as he had done throughout the 1920s,

to be prolific in the publication of pamphlets, articles and reviews, his next, and best known, major work appeared in 1937 as *Political Economy and Capitalism* (Dobb, 1937). For several generations of Dobb's readers, it was the most trenchant critique of its day of the foundations of modern Western economic theory and a long-overdue rehabilitation of the theories of Marx and the classical economists. Dobb, however, was to come to dislike this work, regarding it as too hastily written (Dobb, 1978, p119). Most specifically, he felt its polemics did not adequately assimilate the challenge to orthodox economic theory then being mounted by Keynes and his followers. This became clear to him in discussions with the Polish economist Michal Kalecki, who had arrived at similar theoretical conclusions to those reached by Keynes but by taking as his starting point the schema of reproduction as developed by Marx. Dobb sought to assimilate Kalecki's observations in brief footnotes belatedly added to the second edition of his 1937 volume but these could not rescue it from what Dobb perceived to be its principal deficiencies.

In the 1940s, Dobb's interest in economic history found expression in his seminal contribution to what were to become the internationally influential debates on the transition from feudalism to capitalism. His ideas on this were initially shaped in the discussions of a group of British Marxist historians that included Dona Torr, Christopher Hill and Rodney Hilton. His own historical writing was distinguished by his deployment of Marx's theory of surplus expropriation under different institutional and societal conditions, culminating with the publication of his *Studies in the Development of Capitalism* (op. cit.). As is not infrequent, the entry of a scholar trained in one discipline – in this case economics, and specifically Marxian economics – into another – general history – yielded a new perspective on the subject. For Dobb, Marc Bloch's assessment of the feudal system as one in which the medieval lord 'lived off the labour of other men' wrote on feudalism's face its essential character. Capitalism, by contrast, was a commodity-producing, contractual society ruled by competition. The fact of exploitation was less obvious and had to be explained. For Dobb, Marx had successfully reconciled the existence of surplus value (as the new form of exploitation in capitalist society) with the rule of the market, the 'law of value' and the exchange relationships of universal 'commodity relations' (see McFarlane and Pollitt, 1992, p129). When published, Dobb's *Studies* did not simply influence the approach of a distinguished group of British Marxist social and economic historians but provoked much wider attention, conferring upon him a status and influence far beyond that he ever enjoyed in his own country. This was especially notable in India and Latin America, i.e. in societies that were themselves in various stages of transition from feudalism to capitalism.

The significance of Dobb's work for less industrially developed nations was enhanced with his publication of *Soviet Economic Development since 1917* (op. cit. 1948). In updating his earlier account of Russian development, Dobb was able to portray the transformation of an economy from one that by 1930 had done little more than recover to its levels of 1913 to one that by World War II had manifestly developed a formidable industrial capacity effected under the guidance and control of a national economic plan. For Dobb himself this central feature of the Soviet model of growth seemed:

> likely in turn to become the classic type for the future industrialization of the countries of Asia. Already it has profoundly influenced the discussion of projects for the economic development of India and those for south-eastern Europe. It may well have the effect to-morrow of shifting the focus of economic inquiry; furnishing it with an entirely new set of questions and new perspectives on economic development (ibid, p2).

While critical of various aspects of Dobb's treatment of Soviet economic history, non-Marxian authorities as prestigious as Abram Bergson reported it to be an 'outstanding piece of scholarship and probably the best study of its kind available' (Bergson, 1949). Dobb himself was to think some features of his reportage on Soviet development in the 1930s to have followed Soviet orthodoxies too closely, as is clear from his later writings. Nonetheless, his account of Soviet planning and of the USSR's rapid post-War reconstruction was of special interest in India, and in 1951 he was invited there to deliver a number of lectures.

The 1950s to the 1970s

This visit, however, was to follow a remarkable period in Dobb's academic life in which, while he apparently produced little by his own prolific standards, he was to play a decisive, if barely visible, role in the publication of Piero Sraffa's monumental edition of *The Works and Correspondence of David Ricardo* (Sraffa, 1951-73). Since 1930, at Keynes's instigation, Sraffa had laboured on a project of the Royal Economic Society to publish the complete writings of Ricardo. In 1933, Keynes felt confident enough about its progress to write that Sraffa's 'complete and definitive edition' would be published 'in the course of the present year' (Keynes, 1933, p96). When Keynes died some thirteen years later, however, the edition had still not appeared and Austin Robinson – who had succeeded Keynes as Secretary of the Royal Economic Society – shared a widespread concern as to whether Sraffa would ever be able to submit to the press the edition promised so many years before. Dobb, like Sraffa, was by then a Fellow of Trinity College and, at Robinson's request, began formally to collaborate with Sraffa in what were to prove to be the crucial final stages in completing the edition. A significant factor in the persistent delays in the project lay in the discovery of important new manuscripts that required to be scrutinised and integrated into the edition. More decisive, however, was Sraffa's paralysing perfectionism in both the presentation of Ricardo's writings and in the formulation of his own views as to what these writings signified. Sraffa had lacked confidence in the capability of previous assistants assigned to him and had proved unable to delegate to them even such mundane editorial labours as proof-reading. In the course of collaborative work with Dobb in 1948, however, he became convinced that he could indeed confidently share much of such time-consuming work. More importantly, Dobb broke Sraffa's block in writing down his own thoughts on Ricardo by encouraging him to speak them instead. Dobb would then note them down, probe further, write them up and return them to Sraffa to cogitate upon whether or not they constituted accurate expressions of his thought. This process proved crucial in the writing of the seminal 'Introduction' to Ricardo's *Principles of Political Economy* that was eventually to be published as Volume I of the edition in 1951. In this, Sraffa, in Dobb's view, established that in the history of economic thought, 'the true line of descent is certainly from Ricardo to Marx, and *not* from Ricardo to cost-of-production theory *au* Mill to Marshall as the bourgeois tradition has it' (Pollitt, 1988, p63). This, of course, was vital for Marxists, not least because the 'bourgeois tradition' of which Dobb spoke had thrown out Ricardo's version of the labour theory of value that Marx himself was subsequently to claim and further develop. Dobb's collaborative endeavours continued until the publication of Volume X in 1955 whereupon Austin Robinson wrote to thank him for 'all (his) immense labours' and to deliver himself of the judgement that: 'Without your obstetrical assistance I do not believe that Ricardo would ever have been born' (Pollitt, ibid, p65).

The qualities required of Dobb in this extraordinarily taxing and protracted collaboration with Sraffa were extremely rare. They included: great patience; a deep independent knowledge of Ricardo; a commitment to the most tedious editorial chores as great as to the elucidation and elaboration of grand matters of theory; and the possession of substantial individual creative powers combined with a willingness to suppress their exercise over protracted periods. That Dobb was prepared to deploy all such qualities reflected his perception of a higher interest: one in the final analysis, to be located in a shared, isolated and unfashionable point of entry into the entire arena of political economy and politics (Pollitt, ibid, p64).

With Volume I of the Ricardo edition ready for press by the end of 1951, Dobb embarked on his visit to India, where he lectured extensively on development issues and on the Soviet experience in planning and post-war reconstruction. He delivered three influential lectures at the Delhi School of Economics, two of which were reprinted in his *Papers on Capitalism, Development and Planning* (Dobb, 1967). The lectures clearly reflected his interest in Ricardo's theory of economic growth, and in the fetters to growth – a low growth of productivity in agriculture, financial bottlenecks, and a low rate of profit in industry – that could lead to a 'stationary state'. On returning to Cambridge, he became absorbed once more in work on the Ricardo edition, with the result that the only volume of his own work published between 1948 and 1960 was a selection of earlier lectures or articles entitled *On Economic Theory and Socialism* (Dobb, 1955). Prepared or previously published over three decades from 1924 to 1954, the substance of most of them was to be incorporated into the major works that he published in the same period or later. An exception was his highly regarded article on 'Historical Materialism and the Role of the Economic Factor' (Dobb, 1951), and his concluding, previously unpublished, 'Note on the Transformation Problem'.

The latter was an important summary of the various attempts made by writers such as von Bortkievicz, Winternitz, Sweezy and Kenneth May to resolve what Böhm-Bawerk, at the end of the nineteenth century, had termed the 'Great Contradiction' in Marx. Put simply, in Volume III of *Capital* Marx had acknowledged that exchange under capitalism normally took place at Prices of Production, and he had never satisfactorily demonstrated how these were related to or 'derived' from Values (expressed in terms of embodied labour) as these had been expounded in Volume I. That a key proposition in Marx's Volume III apparently contradicted one in Volume I was enough for Böhm-Bawerk to conclude that: 'The Marxian system has a past and a present, but no abiding future' (Böhm-Bawerk, 1896, p218). It was also enough for economists as notable as Keynes to dismiss *Capital* as unworthy of study, being merely an 'obsolete economic textbook', which Keynes knew (courtesy of Böhm-Bawerk) to be 'scientifically erroneous' (Keynes, 1925, 1931 and cited in Pollitt, op. cit. p59, Note 1). Like Keynes, the great majority of his fellow economists both in the UK and the USA felt it quite unnecessary to read Marx, let alone instruct their students in his theories. A conclusive resolution of the so-called 'Great Contradiction' was hence no trivial matter for Dobb or his fellow Marxists but something that would destroy the theoretical, if not ideological, basis for the disregard in which Marx was held by orthodox Western economists. As will shortly be shown, Dobb seized on Sraffa's later elaboration of what was generally termed a neo-Ricardian model (but which Dobb and others considered equally to be a neo-Marxian one) to clinch the argument in Marx's favour.

Meanwhile, in 1960, Dobb published his own theoretical essay on *Economic Growth and Planning* (Dobb, 1960). In this he sought to give quantitative precision to propositions concerning the rate of investment, the distribution of investment between sectors, and the choice of technique and methods for selecting investment projects in a centrally planned economy. For Dobb, the key investment determinants were, firstly, the productive capacity of the capital goods sector and, secondly, the surplus of production of consumer goods over the self-consumption of the producers in the consumer goods sector; and he advocated a choice of techniques that would maximize economic surplus and growth rather than employment. Dobb's view on this conflicted with the doctrines of comparative cost and marginal productivity, according to which an industrially underdeveloped country with surplus labour must always choose techniques of production which economise on capital. There were strong affinities between Dobb's approach on the choice of techniques and that of A.K. Sen – his research student in Cambridge at that time – but he was primarily influenced by his sympathy for prevailing socialist strategies of development. This work provoked Dobb's only significant dispute with Michal Kalecki who thought – in this writer's view correctly – that Dobb's emphasis on securing a very high rate of investment with correspondingly restricted rates of growth of consumption goods ran the danger of reducing, not increasing, the rate of economic growth by impacting negatively on workers' incentives and therefore productivity.

In 1966, Dobb published an updated edition of his *Soviet Economic Development since 1917* (Dobb, 1966), introducing the discussions on centralised versus decentralised planning methods prompted by the increasingly complex nature of an economy now able to satisfy its most basic consumer needs. His own exposition of the diverse criteria that could be used to guide production and distribution in a developed socialist economy appeared in *Welfare Economics and the Economics of Socialism* (Dobb, 1969). Dobb had lectured on welfare economics and Soviet economic development until his retirement in 1967, and in his 1969 volume he was concerned to expound and differentiate the principles of maximising marginal utility under conditions of perfect competition derived from Walras and Pareto and their followers from the principles discussed and/or deployed in the search for economic optimality in a developed socialist economy.

His final major work reflected Dobb's life-long interest in the history of economic thought and appeared as *Theories of Value and Distribution since Adam Smith* (Dobb, 1973). Its subtitle – *Ideology and economic theory* – reflected Dobb's oft-stated stress on the penetration of ideological judgements into supposedly 'scientific' theoretical propositions, and was a view that proved controversial when he elaborated it in the prestigious Marshall Lectures that he delivered at Cambridge in 1973. The kernel of his argument, as expressed in a letter to W. Brus on 25 July 1973, was that while it 'manages ... to have some positive insights, and hence scientific elements (including of course purely technical aids)', economics, 'since it is a study of historically-developing society', is '*essentially* ideological, in the sense of an artifact of a particular social philosophy and outlook on society...' (Dobb Papers, cited in McFarlane and Pollitt, 1992, op. cit., p132). In his consideration of the development of economic theory from the 1930s, Dobb's long-standing ambivalence about the works of J.M. Keynes – a generally benevolent personal mentor of his since 1924 – was reflected in his sparse treatment of the so-called 'Keynesian Revolution' which he preferred to treat implicitly by focusing on the analogous propositions of Michal Kalecki. His treatment of discussions during the 1960s took as its cornerstone Piero Sraffa's 1960 work on *Production of Commodities by Means of Commodities* (Sraffa, 1960), which, he argued (with others), had destroyed the theoretical foundations of so-called 'neo-classical' theory with its exposure of a logical flaw in the latter's theory of capital. He advanced the view – stemming from his earlier work on Sraffa's edition of Ricardo – that neo-classical theory was inadequate as a macroeconomic theory of production and distribution, and stressed that the connection between this theory and the classical school of thought was a spurious one. It was a source of regret to Dobb that a number of Marxists took what he regarded to be an 'ultra-left' stance towards Ricardo, with factional quarrels between these and the so-called 'neo-Ricardians' impeding what for Dobb – in obviously 'Popular Frontist' mood – would have been the more constructive development of building on Sraffa's 'critique from within' (see, e.g. Dobb 1976A).

MAURICE DOBB ON SOCIALIST ECONOMIC THOUGHT

The brief appraisal given above of Dobb's major publications from 1924 to 1976 serves to indicate both the nature and range of his contributions to political economy and economic history. Translated into many languages, these embraced the theory and practice of development of both capitalism and socialism, the strategies for accelerating the economic growth of the world's poorer countries and the history of economic thought. But they do not include a clear outline of the history of specifically socialist economic thought, or of his own critical perceptions of socialist society as he elaborated these, in particular, during the 1960s and 1970s. We hence offer here a little-known selection of Maurice Dobb's later writings on the development of socialist economic thought and planning.

SOCIALIST THOUGHT

The first essay in this collection is an entry on 'Socialist Thought', written in 1966 and published in 1968 in the *International Encyclopedia of Social Sciences* (Dobb, 1968). For Dobb, any historical account of socialist thought ran predominantly in terms of Marxian doctrine, but he paid sympathetic attention to the philosophical origins and core propositions of pre-Marxian contributions, from the French Utopian socialists of the eighteenth and early nineteenth centuries – notably Saint-Simon, Fourier and Proudhon – to the English Ricardian socialists such as Thompson, Hodgkin, Gray and J.F. Bray. His brief consideration of the German 'Conservative Socialism' of Rodbertus and the popularising activities of Lassalle is followed by a more detailed appraisal of the 'evolutionary' Fabians and of the syndicalist-inspired school of the British Guild Socialists, whose views were a response both to nineteenth century capitalist development and to Marx's own analysis of it.

In his treatment of Marx's doctrine, Dobb links and contrasts it with the contributions of his predecessors in socialist thought, emphasising its philosophical and methodological foundations. He gives a concise exposition of Marx's materialist interpretation of history, in which the distinctive form in which the ruling class appropriated a surplus product from the labouring producer defined the dominant 'mode of production' of the epoch, i.e. slavery, feudal serfdom and modern capitalism, respectively. For Marx, the growing concentration of capital and production into ever-larger units would be accompanied by dislocating economic crises of overproduction and by more extensive and acute class struggles. The explosive outcome would be revolution and socialism, but, as Dobb stresses, both Marx and Engels categorically refused to predict the detailed shape of future socialist society. Their criticism of the Utopian socialists focused precisely on the attempts of these to do this and Marx was particularly concerned, in his *Critique of the Gotha Programme* (Marx, 1876), to stress that the productive powers of any such society – at least in its first or 'lower' stage – would inevitably be limited. This would constrain the emergence of the egalitarian society envisaged by the Utopians and, for Marx, only with the enhanced productive powers and superior moral standards of a 'higher' stage – i.e. communism – could society adopt the egalitarian distributive maxim of 'from each according to his ability, to each according to his needs'.

At the time of the Russian Revolution, there was thus no Marxist blueprint of socialism and it was in its absence that Lenin postulated that the 'bourgeois revolution' of April 1917 could be transformed progressively into a socialist one via an alliance between a minority industrial proletariat and a numerically predominant peasantry.[1] As is shown in Dobb's analysis of Soviet developments in the 1920s – also published in this collection – the political and economic implications of Lenin's thesis were profound.

The Russian Revolution of 1917 was a defining point in the history of socialist thought, with social democracy outside Russia increasingly adopting a 'gradualism' associated most explicitly with British Fabianism. From the late 1940s in particular, there was a retreat from programmes of extensive socialisation of production and this was accompanied by a stress on empirical, rather than theoretical, approaches to socialism. For Dobb, this was best exemplified by the British Labour Party.

Finally, Dobb introduces the debate on the economic principles of socialism, conducted from the last quarter of the nineteenth century (by economists such as Jevons and Menger) through to the reformist discussions in the planned economies of the 1960s (by economists such as Liberman and Ota Šik). This debate is considered more fully in the article that concludes this collection.

THE CENTENARY OF CAPITAL AND ITS RELEVANCE TODAY

First, however, we return to consider a lecture Dobb delivered in March 1967 for the Marx Memorial Library to mark the centenary of the publication of Volume I of *Capital*. This devotes much greater attention than was given in his essay on *Socialist Thought* to Marx's theory of value, and it also provides a more comprehensive account of the nature of the 'Transformation Problem' and of the significance of its various solutions. He considers whether and in what respects there could be any 'reconciliation' between Marx's theories and those of 'modern' or 'bourgeois' economics, and highlights the contrasting rich mingling of concrete historical data with Marx's abstract reasoning – a feature that both resembled and surpassed the method of Adam Smith. Dobb then underlines the importance of integrating an appraisal of *Capital* Volume I with concepts located in Marx's earlier writings on political economy and, more extensively and in more finished form, in the manuscripts painstakingly assembled by Engels and published after Marx's death as *Capital* Volumes II and III. Dobb chooses to express the significance of the latter volumes in particular not in his own words but in those of the iconic figure of Rosa Luxemburg.

THE DISCUSSIONS OF THE 1920S ABOUT BUILDING SOCIALISM

In 1964, Dobb wrote 'The Discussions of the 1920s about Building Socialism' for the Annali of the Istituto Feltrinelli of Milan. Its appearance was delayed but Feltrinelli eventually published it in English in 1967 (Dobb, 1967).

This was not Dobb's first account of the debate among Soviet economists in the 1920s. He had reported much of it contemporaneously, as it unfolded during his first visit to Moscow in 1925 and subsequently as he prepared his book on *Russian Economic Development since the Revolution* (loc. cit). This appeared in two editions in 1928, the second concluding with an Appendix, 'On Agriculture and Industry in 1927-28', which summarised the key problems of socialist accumulation in a predominantly peasant economy as these were identified by Soviet economists on the eve of the First Five-Year Plan.

The Soviet debate focused upon one complex issue. Rapid industrialisation was thought essential for social, economic and political reasons. The problem, however, lay in determining the rate and type of industrial growth that should be sought given the key constraint to be the marketed surplus of peasant agriculture. If higher rates of industrialisation depended on the extraction of larger surpluses from agriculture – for more urban food supplies, industrial raw materials and exports – what methods would most effectively secure them? For example, should peasant production as a whole be stimulated by improvements in the terms of trade between agriculture and industry? Or should price and tax mechanisms be used to squeeze the peasants – particularly the 'rich' peasants or kulaks – to surrender a greater share of their harvests? Such questions were not narrow economic ones, for the policies chosen could strengthen or weaken social classes or strata perceived as both more and less supportive of the revolutionary regime. And for the Soviet leadership at the time, there was a pervasive, frustrating perception that the economic progress of the whole nation rested not so much on the decision-making powers of socialist planners as on those of an atomised peasantry.

It was fortuitous that Dobb's early account of all this was concluded and published in 1928. Open Soviet debate of these matters ended shortly thereafter with the adoption of the First Five-Year Plan and the unleashing of the forced collectivisation of agriculture at the end of 1929. Official Soviet historiography later suppressed or distorted earlier discussions. Worse, many of the principal protagonists – whether 'Leftist' or 'Rightist' – were anathematised and executed in the purges of the 1930s. In 1948, Dobb published his *Soviet Economic Development since 1917* (loc. cit). In this major work, he was supportive both of the strategy and planning methods used to accelerate Soviet industrial growth during the 1930s, but his account of the 1920s discussions drew largely upon the contemporaneous treatment he had himself published twenty years before. This was important, for while he said nothing about the ultimate fate of figures such as Bukharin or Preobrazensky, their official anathematisation did not disfigure his exposition of their contributions to the debates of the 1920s.

Dobb's treatment of these debates, as written in 1964 and reproduced in the present selection, was partly prompted and shaped by political and intellectual events of the 1950s. In the first place, Khrushchev's denunciation of Stalin at the Soviet Communist Party's Twentieth Congress in 1956, together with the popular uprisings in Hungary and Poland that followed it, forced Dobb to reconsider his view both of the Soviet past and the East European present. The rocky Soviet path of economic growth followed in the 1930s had then been proclaimed to be not one, but 'the' road of socialist construction. Dobb looked afresh at the events of the 1920s, partly to see whether hindsight illuminated feasible alternative routes. Secondly, World War II had weakened the grasp of the European imperial powers on their Asian, African and Caribbean colonies. Dozens of emerging, formally independent nations now sought to accelerate the processes of economic growth. A growing number of Western economists, hitherto preoccupied with the workings of developed capitalism, now turned their attention to the more elemental problems of this new, so-called 'Third World'. To the extent that their theories were informed (often implicitly) by historical experience, this was generally that of capitalism, and this was reflected in the strategies of economic growth that they advocated. The fashionable 'textile road' to development, for example, pursued within capitalist property relations and ostensibly governed by the market, had both empirical and ideological roots in Britain's industrial revolution of the eighteenth and nineteenth centuries. But there was a conspicuous, radically different and apparently successful alternative to all this. It was not export-orientated light industry or *laissez-faire* capitalism that had transformed the USSR from a predominantly agrarian nation into an industrial and military superpower. The Soviet growth process had instead been distinguished by the planned priority given to the development of heavy industry, with the 'commanding heights' of the whole economy in public ownership and control.

In the 1950s and after, the growth processes of what was variously described as the under-, less-, or mis-developed world were analysed within the fraught geo-political context of the Cold War. Poorer countries sought faster transitions to development than those experienced by the capitalist economies held up for them as examples. Economists of the industrially developed world identifying the 'obstacles to growth' of poor countries had hence to proffer strategies enabling these to be overcome with acceptable speed. Little light was cast on the problem by the corpus of economic theory then prevailing in capitalist countries since this was more concerned with static and cyclical than dynamic conditions.

Moreover, crucial development problems were often defined as 'externalities' and as such were excluded from the very province of theoretical analysis. Most economists seeking to identify the primary long-run determinants of economic growth, whether institutional or 'technical', had thus to return to the preoccupations of classical economists such as Smith and Ricardo. Their journey was made more difficult by their ignorance of the Soviet debate of the 1920s that had addressed so many analogous problems. Furthermore, most seemed unaware of elementary analytical categories used by Marx and drawn on later by some of his more creative followers to illuminate problems of both less- and more developed countries. As a result, some of the 'pioneers' of the development theories published in the West from the 1950s 'discovered' lands that had already been mapped with considerable intellectual distinction. This became more widely, if not universally, appreciated in the course of the 1960s, as a growing number of translations and interpretations of some of the path-breaking contributions of the early Soviet economists made these more generally accessible.[2]

PLANNING

In the western development literature of the 1950s and after, a measure of state intervention was commonly advocated to accelerate the growth processes of 'emerging' nations. At the time, this was hardly heretical.[3] Various forms and degrees of state economic management had by then become commonplace within the principal capitalist countries, initially as a response to the exigencies of the Great Depression and, more prominently, during World War II and its aftermath.

In the arena of fiscal and monetary policy, the so-called 'Keynesian revolution' had overthrown the doctrine that the best government was the least government; and in countries poorly endowed with the physical and institutional infrastructure judged propitious for economic development, it was obvious that the State could play a more directly constructive role. These, and a myriad of other state activities designed to shape the pattern of economic growth, were commonly sheltered under the umbrella term of 'development planning' or, simply, 'planning'.

Dobb made significant contributions of his own to planning theory and practice,[4] but we publish here the original English version of his overview of 'Planning', written in 1972 and published only in translation, shortly after his death in 1976, in the *Enciclopedia Italiana* (Rome, 1976B).

As Dobb makes plain, the idea of economic planning was first formulated, in vague and general terms, by the nineteenth century pioneers of socialist thought. Even Marx and Engels spoke no more than of producers or production being 'regulated' according to some predetermined but unspecified general 'plan'. That any such plan could allocate resources efficiently was disputed, in the early twentieth century, by writers such as von Mises, the latter arguing, in strikingly familiar terms, that: 'Where there is no free market, there is no pricing mechanism; without a pricing mechanism, there is no economic calculation' (see p121). This was challenged in the West in the 1930s by Marxian economists who took up the question of whether or not socialist planning could deal with variations in the supply and demand of goods or 'productive factors'. Their discussion included the roles that interest-rates and enterprise 'accounting prices' might play in securing an efficient allocation of resources – subjects which, as Dobb pointed out, implicitly raised the question that was to dominate debate in the political economy of socialism from the late 1950s onwards. This, of course, concerned the conditions in which centralised or decentralised planning mechanisms, of diverse kinds and in varied combinations, best served the interests of economic efficiency and general social well-being.

In discussing planning under capitalist conditions, Dobb summarised the theoretical difficulties of reconciling 'market' criteria of 'efficiency' with wider concerns with social welfare and, hence, with the distribution of income – questions he had himself discussed in the 1930s. But in more practical terms, he was clearly doubtful whether the 'indicative' planning methods in vogue after World War II, and which sought to 'steer' or 'guide' capitalist production, really constituted planning properly so-called. In his view, as expressed in the various editions of his *Soviet Development since 1917*, there were two preconditions for effective economic planning.

The first was adequate knowledge of the internal relationships between the constituent elements of the economy, the conscious use of which:

> amounts to the attempt to substitute *ex ante* coordination of (these) in a scheme of development for the tardy *post facto* coordinating tendencies that are operated by the mechanism of price movements on a market in a capitalist world – tendencies, moreover, which in the presence of substantial time-lags may merely achieve extensive fluctuations. In this the essential difference between a planned economy and an unplanned evidently consists (*ibid*, pp8-9).

Secondly, positive *ex ante* planning implied social, not private, ownership of the key productive sectors, since:

> [the] crucial obstacle to any attempt to impose a set of centralised decisions upon a capitalist economy is the tendency of entrepreneurs, who still hold (or until recently held) rights of economic sovereignty, to obstruct any provisions of an economic plan which run counter to the aim of maximising the profit to be earned upon their property ... In such circumstances an economic plan imposed upon the economy from above is likely to have a purely negative character, excluding certain courses of action from the agenda or setting limits within which the autonomous decisions of entrepreneur units can operate (ibid, p30).

It followed from all this that, for Dobb, the study of economic planning was primarily an examination of the planning systems that emerged, firstly, in the USSR and, later, in the economies of Eastern Europe. We have already seen that Soviet political economy in the 1920s was dominated by controversy as to the feasible tempo and type of economic growth that could or should be planned. Partly as a result, there was then neither a clearly identifiable system of planning nor a coherent medium- or long-term national plan. But as the 1920s came to a close, discussion of alternative development strategies was ended with the definitive adoption of the first of several Five-Year Plans that pursued extraordinarily high rates of growth of industry in general and of heavy industry in particular. The early Five-Year Plans – like the political and administrative systems that implemented them – were highly centralised and, initially at least, endeavoured to control much operational detail. But in the tumultuous circumstances of the time, a centralised planning system of this kind could in practice pursue only priorities, and the planners shifted resources from one economic front to another much as military strategists moved men and materiel from one front to another in time of war.

Military metaphors of this kind were often deployed by Dobb to illuminate Soviet planning in what was sometimes called its 'heroic' period, and the image of human and other resources being amassed to force open productive bottlenecks and smash or 'storm' through obstacles evoked the Soviet reality of the times far more effectively than an analysis couched solely in the mundane terms of economic accounting. The content of Soviet plans in the 1930s and 1940s, and the methodology of planning itself, were inevitably in flux. Simple trial and error led to significant changes both in plan targets and in the ways in which their pursuit was calculated. National and international emergencies – most conspicuously World War II and its aftermath – forced major adjustments in planning objectives. But a persistent central feature of Soviet planning throughout these turbulent years was the use of 'priority-lists' of economic objectives.

Within the 'priority-list' system, shortfalls in the resources required to fulfil highly-ranked sectoral plans could be met by tapping those initially assigned to plans of lower rank. In practice, given the conditions of the time, this meant that resources allocated for the increased production of consumer-goods were commonly diverted to bolster plans to expand the producer-goods sector, particularly where this was linked to national defence capabilities.

The simplicity of such a system was a cardinal virtue during the 'heroic' period of planning and growth but, by the end of the post-1945 reconstruction period, its defects had become increasingly apparent. Soviet growth up to the 1950s was essentially 'extensive' in nature, being fuelled primarily by the simple addition of labour and means of production to existing productive capacity. With the exhaustion of abundant reserves of labour in particular, however, it became obvious that future growth would have to be more 'intensive' in character, and originate in rising productivity *per capita.*

Clearly, this could be achieved only by technical progress and an improved organisation and efficiency of an economy that had become increasingly complex and increasingly capable of satisfying the population's basic needs. In the Soviet conditions of the time, a successful transition from 'extensive' to 'intensive' patterns of growth could hardly be determined by central administrative *fiat.* While there was an obvious need for technical innovations – to widen the range and improve the quality of consumer goods, for example – a palpable bureaucratic and managerial inertia could check the speed and effectiveness with which these were promoted or adopted at the point of production. As important was the enthusiasm, or lack of it, of enterprise management and labour for organisational changes designed to eliminate wasteful work-practices. The latter were for the most part easily identified, but they were also highly intractable. This was for the good reason that enterprises had actively colluded to create many of them in the first place, principally to take advantage of inadequacies in the 'performance indicators' set by the centre to measure the fulfilment of production plans and determine the distribution of profits within the enterprises. Given problems such as these, reformers argued that a social and productive *milieu* in which both management and labour would work notably harder and better could be created only with the progressive de-centralisation of planning and administration.

The desirable nature and extent of de-centralisation was debated in the USSR and Eastern Europe from the 1950s onwards, and Dobb's account of this in 'Planning' was characteristically judicious. The restraint with which he discussed some of the issues, however, tended to obscure the strength and sharpness of the views he himself had by then come to hold on the subject – views that were insufficiently appreciated by readers familiar only with the more narrowly economic of Dobb's writings as published in the academic press.

In the late 1940s, Dobb undertook the first of a series of visits to Eastern Europe that he was to continue through the 1950s and 1960s. In the course of these, he usually lectured on recent developments in 'Western' – or, in Moscow in 1966, 'bourgeois' – economic theory for the benefit of academic audiences, most often in Prague, Budapest and Warsaw. At the same time, however, he familiarised himself with the discussions on economic reform then being conducted among his hosts. At the time, this subject tended to be treated in muted, if not coded, terms in official East European publications, but over the years, in England as well as in Eastern Europe, Dobb had formed his own personal and intellectual ties with reformers such as Michal Kalecki and Wlodimir Brus in Poland, or Ota Šik in Czechoslovakia. His understanding of their positions, as of those of prominent reformers in Hungary and the GDR, was thus honed in first-hand discussions and often complemented by correspondence. He was unenthusiastic about changes that he thought might weaken control over the basic structure of investment or significantly cut its overall rate,[5] but, this apart, he generally sided with the reformers in arguing the case for de-centralisation.[6] The political and social imperatives of economic reform were forcefully brought home to him in Poland at the end of June 1956, when a visit to Poznan coincided with violent popular riots. (He gathered, and carefully conserved his 'Poznan Mementos': machine-pistol cartridge cases that he picked up in the street, together with fragments of insulators shot off telephone poles.) A few days later, he was able to discuss these events in Warsaw with Kalecki, among others, and in 1965, albeit in typically understated form, he reported their personal impact upon him in his 'Random Biographical Notes', written for a Polish audience in 1965 and published posthumously in 1978 (Dobb, 1978). When Soviet tanks brought an icy end to Dubcek's 'Prague Spring' in August 1968, Dobb's views markedly hardened, and this was reflected in the vigour of his advocacy of political and economic reform in Eastern Europe and in the growing harshness with which he referred to its opponents.

Soviet intervention in Czechoslovakia in 1968 brought to a head internal disputes that had simmered within Western European Communist Parties for more than a decade. In his own Party's press in 1956, Dobb himself had censured the 'heel-clicking' support for Soviet intervention in Hungary then given by the leadership of the British CP, and he was a signatory of critical letters that the CP press refused to publish and which were therefore published elsewhere.[7] While he appeared to be in a minority for some years thereafter in pressing the case for reform in Eastern Europe, this was to change in the course of the 1960s as a growing number of western Communist Parties modified their hitherto unconditional support for the regimes of the Soviet bloc and adopted a more critical stance. This revision of traditional appraisals was generally discreet because most CP leaderships were apprehensive of exacerbating internal and international Party divisions.

The British CP was a case in point. By the mid-1960s, most of its leaders had come to hold the view that both political and economic reforms were desirable in Eastern Europe but this became publicly apparent only with their enthusiastic support for the far-reaching reform programme that the Czechoslovak Communist Party sought to implement up to August 1968. But even this support was circumspect, for Czechoslovakia was suggested to be something of a special case, with particularly propitious conditions for its endeavours to create 'Socialism with a Human Face'.

It was pointed out that, unlike other countries in eastern Europe, Czechoslovakia was relatively developed industrially when it entered the Soviet bloc in 1948 and possessed a substantial and politically sophisticated urban working class. Unlike Hungary or Romania it had not been one of the Axis Powers during World War II, and in contrast to Poland or East Germany, it had no obvious anti-Russian or anti-Soviet popular tradition. Finally, while its history as an independent state was brief, it had been marked by a political pluralism unusual in the Soviet bloc. In short, it was implied that Czechoslovakia was not really an 'eastern' country at all, but a 'western' one; and Communist Parties throughout western Europe followed the progress of Dubcek's political and economic reforms with intense interest, hoping for a model of 'existing' socialism with which they (and their prospective domestic supporters) could more fully empathise. Ruling CPs in east European countries and the USSR, however, viewed the reform process in Czechoslovakia in quite a different light. They feared that it would strengthen unwanted imitative pressures within their own boundaries, eventually adducing a threat to the security of the entire Warsaw Pact to justify its suppression by Soviet-led forces in August 1968.

The military occupation of Czechoslovakia, and the installation in Prague of a puppet regime enjoying the scantiest popular support, had an obvious and intended intimidatory impact within other east European countries. But it also destroyed a model of an emerging 'democratic' socialism that had enthused many Communist Parties in the west, while seeming to confirm Soviet intolerance for any authentically autonomous national 'road to socialism'. The combination forced many 'fraternal parties' to condemn Soviet action in terms that were unprecedented in their scope and severity. This in turn brought out into the open the increasingly bitter battles being fought within them between, on the one hand, critics of Soviet intervention and of the Soviet-style model of socialism more generally, and, on the other, the more unconditional pro-Soviet loyalists.

The British CP leadership's criticism of Soviet intervention was supported by a comfortable majority of its members but the opposition to it included personalities who had been prominent in the shaping of Party policy since the 1920s and 1930s. Foremost among these was Rajani Palme Dutt[8] – a forbidding figure with whom Dobb had had an uneasy relationship since the early 1930s. At that time, before it championed the antifascist Popular Front, the British CP had set itself the task of exposing the 'social fascism' of the Labour Party and, in a little-known episode that was symptomatic of the high sectarianism of those years, Dutt and others appeared to seek at the least to break Dobb, if not to drive him out of the Party altogether, by savaging a booklet he published in 1932 entitled *On Marxism To-day* (Dobb, 1932). This was portrayed in *The Daily Worker* as having 'nothing to do with Marxism' and Dobb was lambasted for writing 'from above the battle'.[9] His attempt to defend himself in that newspaper was rebutted yet more forcefully, when he was charged with the 'positive distortion of the fundamentals of Marxism in every field'. It was alleged that his 'economic errors' in particular could 'be traced through all his writings' and his treatment of political struggle earned the deadly characterisation of being 'exactly the Social-Democratic position'.[10]

Meanwhile, Dutt himself delivered a contemptuous *ex cathedra* rebuke to a certain type of 'bourgeois intellectual' – among whom Dobb was undoubtedly to be numbered – in the *Communist Review*. According to Dutt, an intellectual within the Communist Party should 'first and foremost ... *forget that he is an intellectual* (except in moments of necessary self criticism) *and remember only that he is a* Communist' (Dutt, 1932).[11]

Finally, and for Dobb most unpleasant of all, an attempt was made to bring him to heel in his own CP Branch in Cambridge. Here a special subcommittee was set up to consider the *Daily Worker's* censures of the offending booklet and, on 10 August 1932, an aggregate meeting passed a resolution calling upon him to repudiate publicly his 'idealist and opportunist perversion of Marxism' – a perversion attributed to lack of the 'stimulus and correcting influence' provided only by 'continued contact with the revolutionary proletariat'. Dobb defended himself vigorously; refused to recant; and, unlike some of the signatories of the resolution in question,[12] remained a committed Marxist and Communist Party member until his death. While he never publicly referred to his 1932 experiences,[13] it was nonetheless evident that they wounded him deeply. In the years that followed, he neglected his scholarly work, heightening instead his practical political activity (Dobb, 1978, p19) and the phraseology of some of his later writings bore the marks of an obvious and painfully inculcated caution.

The wary apprehension with which Dobb viewed Dutt in the 1930s had developed by the 1960s into a quiet hostility for a figure he privately thought to be an arrogant dogmatist of almost messianic pretensions. When Dutt emerged as the principal ideologue opposing the British CP's condemnation of Soviet intervention in Czechoslovakia in 1968, he represented for Dobb all that was retrograde in the political and ideological history of his Party.[14]

The crushing of the Czechoslovak reform programme brought to a halt wider decentralising trends that had been observable in Eastern Europe and within the USSR itself since the mid-1960s. In Dobb's eyes, while these trends had been slow and halting, they had nonetheless been preconditions for the economic and political revitalisation of socialism, and he doubted the stability of systems that resisted yet more comprehensive processes of decentralisation. He stated this unequivocally in 1970 in a popular work on *Socialist Planning: Some Problems* (Dobb, 1970). There is no doubt that, like the vast majority of other well-informed observers, Dobb would have been astonished at the speed and extent of the collapse of east European regimes from 1989, let alone of the implosion of the USSR itself from 1991. Nonetheless, there was a certain prescience in the passage with which he concluded his 1970 booklet:

What the direction and degree of future change will be is impossible at the moment to forecast with any assurance. In some major respects one could say that socialist planning and administration at the outset of the 1970s stands at the crossroads. To-date the direction of change has undoubtedly been towards greater decentralization. But in the Soviet Union, at least, there might well be a halt, and even a conservative drawing back to the limited degree of economic reform at which Poland and East Germany (DDR) seem for the present to have become stabilized. That this will prove a stable halting place seems unlikely: more likely that (problems previously discussed) will impel further decentralizing measures eventually, in a search for a more complete and rounded reform. What well may be decisive, however, is not the economic results *per se* but the social objectives involved. In other words, the question of which direction is taken is even more a political than it is an economic question ...: concerned as it is with the degree of democracy to be achieved and the amount of participation of individual workers, on the one hand, and of individual consumers, on the other, in deciding the manner in which and the ends towards which the system of production operates. Even if there be signs of a freezing of bureaucratic structures since the setback to reform in Czechoslovakia in 1968-9, it is hardly likely that the new technological age and higher living standards can be contained within the old administrative mould inherited from Stalin's day. Economic problems sometimes acquire a compelling logic of their own. One may well see some rapidly changing alignments and landmarks in the socialist world in the decade that lies ahead (pp68-9).

COMMODITY-PRODUCTION UNDER SOCIALISM

The concluding paper in this edition was read to a seminar organised by the Committee for the Study of European Socialist Countries at Cambridge in May 1976. Entitled 'Commodity-Production under Socialism', it was delivered three months before Dobb's death, and was transcribed from his manuscript notes and published posthumously in the short-lived journal *Socialist Europe* (Dobb, 1976C). Dobb here addressed the fundamental question of whether and why Marx's 'first stage of socialism' is compatible or incompatible with the existence of commodity-production or market relations. Dobb rooted his discussion in the Soviet experience of the 1920s and, in his review of the subsequent development of socialist economy, he took the opportunity to indicate how some of his own views had modified since his first major engagement with the subject in *Russian Economic Development since the Revolution* (Dobb, 1928). He was concerned in particular to look again at the significance of the period of the 'New Economic Policy' (NEP) of 1921, arguing that while this was powerfully shaped by Russia's economic backwardness and the preponderance of the peasantry, it nonetheless embodied elements essential to a socialist economy in its first or 'lower' stages, which should not have been discarded as comprehensively as they were in the 'retreat from NEP' of the 1930s. The experience of the 1950s and 1960s showed, for Dobb, that while planning may control 'key' products, producers' goods should generally be distributed by free contracting between enterprises. And so long as there was wage-payment according to labour and insufficient supply, a retail market for consumers' goods was essential to afford consumers choice. Dobb notes that the 1970s discussion of Hungary's so-called 'new economic mechanisms' featured a re-exploration of the Soviet NEP.[15] One might add that in the later 1980s, parallels were also drawn between the NEP and the belated (and in the event implosive) process of political and economic reforms initiated in the USSR under Gorbachev.[16] It may be that in part this reflected a desire to give a legitimating ideological lineage to reforms that could be interpreted as retreats from 'real' socialism. But it also reflected the richness of Soviet debate and experience of socialist economy in its formative years, which could stimulate fruitful discussion, within Marxian terms of reference, for many decades thereafter.

THE FUTURE OF PLANNING

In the event, of course, in the 1990s, command of the economies of eastern Europe and of the USSR/CIS was seized by forces who were generally either ignorant of, or antithetical towards, the intellectual legacies of the founding fathers of the modern political economy of socialism, and who preferred a *tabula rasa* upon which to inscribe the dogmas of an atavistic model of western capitalism. The principles as well as the (often ossified) practices of socialist planning were now denigrated, as was Marxist doctrine as a whole. The new politico-economic model was claimed to be that of the 'free market' functioning within Western-style 'democracy'. But in reality what emerged to replace the old system was often based on the lowest common denominator of populist ideology, namely nationalist, ethnic and religious passions; and these provoked destructive conflicts both within and between European and Asian nation states in the post-Soviet era.

In post-1991 Russia, successive political regimes were sustained by an economic oligarchy created by the corrupt, cheap and commonly criminalised sale of economic assets previously owned by the Soviet state. Portrayed as 'free market liberalisation', the 'shock' dismantling of the Soviet system of state economic and social planning brought with it a precipitate decline in national income and employment, a spectacular growth in income inequalities and a stark increase in mortality rates. At the same time, the accompanying weakening of Russian state power was brought into sharper and more humiliating focus by the over-weaning geopolitical ambitions of the US, especially as expressed in Washington's policies towards Eastern Europe. The Russian state sought to re-assert its influence both at home and abroad via its recapture of ownership of, or control over, a growing share of the nation's most potent material assets, namely the extraction, processing and transshipment of oil and gas. Out of an anarchic, so-called 'laissez faire' economy with a weakened state – belittled and patronised by a triumphalist US – there hence grew a bourgeoning new 'state capitalism', that permitted Russia's perceived national interests to be projected with greater vigour.

To what new ordering of the world's political and economic affairs all this will lead is uncertain. The longstanding dominance of the opposing camps of Western capitalism and Soviet-style socialism has ended, but Cold War victory did not bring the unchallenged global hegemony assumed by successive US administrations and epitomised in a pronouncement of the 'end of history'. The rival growth of China's global influence, for example, promises to be spectacular, albeit resting on the paradoxical coexistence of a barely-bridled capitalist expansionism alongside the continuing exercise of national and international state political power by an ambitious Communist Party. In Latin America, on the other hand, a so-called 'pink tide' of regimes in the US 'backyard' have declared themselves, if not for revolutionary socialism, then at least as advocates of greatly increased state ownership or control of national energy and other national resources that were previously in the exclusive hands of US and/or European interests.

In fact, the supposedly hegemonic model of the 'Western free market' economy has been challenged by a plethora of alternative variants. Most of these have assigned a prominent role in economic management to the state. Resources judged to be of strategic importance for national social and economic development have been nationalised (or re-nationalised), and previously unchecked activities of capitalist multinationals have been constrained by direct state involvement in joint ventures and/or in the imposition of production controls and taxation systems.

A powerful contemporary incentive for more vigorous state intervention and for diverse forms of national planning has been the menacing global threat of climate change. 'Free market' economies in the industrially developed world – most conspicuously in the US itself – have proved excessively tardy in both the conservation and cleaner and more efficient use of scarce fossil fuels, and the initiatives of private enterprise in the development of alternative ways to generate energy have been feeble. And it is self-evidently the logic of international capitalism that drives unsustainable consumerism of all kinds.

The environmental record of Soviet planning was, of course, appalling, but this did not reflect any specific property of planning mechanisms *per se.* It reflected, rather, the excessive priority given over many decades to high-tempo industrial growth regardless of its wider environmental impact. But such a negative historical precedent does not weaken the proposition that the state is manifestly able to perceive social costs – such as environmental degradation – that fall outside the concerns of economic enterprises (whether private or state-run), which are ruled by ambitions to maximise profitability and/or productivity to the neglect of criteria external to 'the market', whether this be local, national or global.

Hence state intervention and diverse forms of national economic planning and control are emerging from the 'dustbin of history' to which they were consigned by ideologists of the 'free market'. They may be deployed for a variety of goals: the alleviation of unacceptable levels of inequality and mass poverty; to reduce or control foreign exploitation of scarce or strategically vital national resources; to mitigate harsh fluctuations in income and employment caused by the volatility of international markets; and to regulate a myriad of activities that threaten the balance of an increasingly precarious global environment. In such a context, the study of the history, theory and practice of socialist planning is a fruitful one, assisting us to evaluate both more and less promising means with which to pursue desirable social ends.

NOTES

1. Lenin's view was controversial in the history of Marxist thought because it asserted that socialism could be built in a society where capitalism (and with it the industrial proletariat) had not yet been fully developed. While Dobb does not make the point, Mao's revolution in China, together with less significant examples elsewhere in Asia, Africa and Latin America, were all underpinned by variations of Lenin's theoretical position.
2. Significant among these was Alexander Erlich's *The Soviet Industrialisation Debate, 1924-28* (1960); N. Spulber's edition of Soviet economic essays for the period 1924-30, translated in *Foundations of Soviet Economic Growth* (1964); Brian Pearce's translation of Preobrazhensky's *The New Economics* (1965); and Thorner, Kerblay and Smith's edition of Chayanov's *The Theory of Peasant Economy* (1966). Joan Robinson noted how ignorance of the reproduction schema deployed by Marx in Vol. II of *Capital* had obliged the early Keynesians to reinvent an important theoretical wheel by imagining a cordon drawn round the capital-goods industries and then studying the trade between them and the consumption-good industries (Robinson, 1964). The affinity between the famous Harrod-Domar growth model and the work of 1928 to 1929 of G.A. Feldman (see Dobb in the present edition, p112, Notes 51-3, p118) was acknowledged, albeit somewhat condescendingly, by Domar himself (Domar, 1957), Feldman's model itself being developed from Marx's reproduction schema. And in 1968, Michal Kalecki analysed Marx's reproduction models and contemporary growth models (Kalecki, 1968).
3. The notion that direct state intervention was both important and necessary to promote development in poor countries was, of course, vigorously disputed, particularly at the height of the Cold

War. W.W. Rostow's *Stages of Economic Growth* (1960), for example, was subtitled *An Anti-Communist Manifesto* and argued that the experience of modern industrial nations revealed a general sequence of stages in their development. This was substantially independent of variations in their social structures, and state planning that sought to transform these was therefore redundant. A.O. Hirschman reported evocatively on the ideological sensitivity of literature on development planning when he noted the preference of a Washington friend that his own book on *The Strategy of Economic Development* (1958), be mimeographed rather than printed, with 'its distribution limited to a few sophisticated officials and experts directly concerned with economic development' (Preface to the Paperbound Edition, pvii).

4. See, for example, the selection of essays published in *On Economic Theory and Socialism* (Dobb, 1955); *Economic Growth and Planning* (Dobb, 1960); *Papers on Capitalism, Development and Planning* (Dobb, 1967, sections 3-5); *Welfare Economics and the Economics of Socialism* (Dobb, 1969, Part 11); and *Socialist Planning: Some Problems* (Dobb, 1970).
5. For example, Dobb generally espoused the approach elaborated by G.A. Feldman in the USSR in the late 1920s. Feldman's model pointed to the long-run growth-accelerating virtues of allocating a high proportion of total investment to the producer-goods sector. Michal Kalecki, by contrast, stressed that an insufficient allocation of resources to current consumer-goods production could have a negative impact on the long-run rate of growth by depressing the efficiency of labour (see T. Kowalik, 1964, pp10-11.)
6. Dobb' s relations with prominent reformist economists in Eastern Europe was reflected both by the award of an honorary doctorate of economic science at the Charles University of Prague in 1964, and by the blocking, at a political level, of an attempt by Brus, Kalecki and Lange to secure him a similar honour in Poland. (Details of the Polish case were provided to this writer by B. J. McFarlane, who interviewed Ada Kalecki and T. Kowalik in Warsaw.) Dobb was made an Honorary Member of the Hungarian Academy of Sciences in 1973.
7. See entry on 'Maurice Dobb' (McFarlane and Pollitt, 1992, p133); and Hobsbawm, 1986, p19.
8. See *Rajani Palme Dutt: a Study in British Stalinism* (Callaghan, 1993).
9. *Daily Worker*, 10 June 1932.

10. *Daily Worker*, 26 July 1932. Dobb's critic was Hugo Rathbone, who was well known at the time as 'one of Palme Dutt's assistants as guardian of Party orthodoxy' (see Macintyre, 1980, p121).
11. Dutt was particularly contemptuous of a project for leading Communist intellectuals to organise themselves into groups reflecting their professional specialisms, reporting that this had been 'nipped in the bud' by Party headquarters (Branson 1985, pp205-06). This measure, *inter alia*, delayed the formation of the influential CP Historians' Group for more than a decade.
12. The subcommittee's report and the resolution echoing its various charges, together with Dobb's speech of defence, were found among his other Papers in 1983 and are lodged in Trinity College as DOBB CC2 (38-42). It was found that Dobb had protected the identity of the various authors and signatories by deleting their names from the documents. The Marxist philosopher Maurice Cornforth, who was a long standing friend and political associate of Dobb's, was present at the 1932 Cambridge meeting. When interviewed by this writer in 1983, he accounted for Dobb's censorship by pointing out that at least one prominent signatory had later been killed in the Spanish Civil War.
13. Eric Hobsbawm wrote a biographical introduction to the *Festschrift* of essays on *Socialism, Capitalism & Economic Growth* (1967) presented to Dobb on his retirement. He referred there to his own youthful encounter with Dobb's *On Marxism To-Day* just two years after its publication in 1932, but he was then and later quite unaware of the painful inner-CP *furore* this small but influential booklet had provoked at the time and, hence, of an important cause of Dobb's cautious public demeanour in later years.
14. In 1970, Dobb's friend Tedy Prager left the Austrian CP after its pro-Soviet faction carried the day at a Party Congress. Dobb described this as 'one less hope for eventual vanquishing of the hosts of darkness' and Prager's decision as a problem he would have had to face himself 'if the Duttites had won at our last Congress – as I personally feared seriously that they might do...'. He agreed that up to August 1968 'one cd. be optimistic and say that at least there was movement in the right direction, if slow, halting, uneven. Now one can no longer say this – and any movement there may be is in the wrong direction – back again to the intolerable past' (letter to T. Prager, 3 March 1970, Trinity College Library, DOBB CB19 (136-7)).

15. See, e.g. L. Szamuely, 1974.
16. Gorbachev's own *Perestroika – New Thinking for our Country and the World* (1987, p25) claimed Lenin as a major ideological source of *perestroika*, most particularly with his stress on recognising the 'requirements of "objective" economic laws, on planning and cost accounting, and intelligent use of commodity-money relations and material and moral incentives'. The CPSU's adoption in 1987 of 'Fundamentals of Radical Restructuring of Economic Management' was described by Gorbachev as perhaps 'the most important and radical economic reform our country has had since Lenin introduced his New Economic Policy in 1921' (ibid, p33).

Brian Pollitt, spring 2008

BIBLIOGRAPHY

A. Bergson, 1949, *New Republic*, 7 March.
E. von Böhm-Bawerk, 1896, *Karl Marx and the Close of his System*, translated by A.M. Macdonald, London.
N. Branson, 1985, *History of the Communist Party of Great Britain, 1927-1941*, London: Lawrence & Wishart.
J. Callaghan, 1993, *Rajani Palme Dutt: a Study in British Stalinism*, London: Lawrence & Wishart.
A.V. Chayanov, 1966, *The Theory of Peasant Economy*, translated and edited by Thorner, Kerblay and Smith, Homewood, Illinois.
E. Domar, 1957, *Essays in the Theory of Economic Growth*, New York: OUP.
M.H. Dobb, 1925, *Capitalist Enterprise and Social Progress*, London: Routledge.
M.H. Dobb, with the assistance of H.C. Stevens, 1928A, *Russian Economic Development since the Revolution*, London: Labour Research Department and Routledge.
M.H. Dobb, 1928B, *Wages*, Cambridge: CUP.
M.H. Dobb, 1932A, *An Introduction to Economics*, London: Gollancz.
M.H. Dobb, 1932B, *Marxism To-day*, London: Hogarth Press.
M.H. Dobb, 1937, *Political Economy and Capitalism*, London: Routledge.
M.H. Dobb, 1946, *Studies in the Development of Capitalism*, London: Routledge.

M.H. Dobb, 1948, revised edition 1966, *Soviet Economic Development since 1917*, London: Routledge & Kegan Paul.

M.H. Dobb, 1951, 'Historical Materialism and the Role of the Economic Factor', *History*, February and June.

M.H. Dobb, 1955, *On Economic Growth and Socialism*, London: Routledge & Kegan Paul.

M.H. Dobb, 1960, *Economic Growth and Planning*, London, Routledge & Kegan Paul.

M.H. Dobb, 1967, 'The Discussions of the 1920s about Building Socialism', *Annali*, Milan: Istituto Giangiacomo Feltrinelli.

M.H. Dobb, 1968, 'Socialist Thought', in D.L. Sills (ed.), *International Encyclopedia of Social Sciences*, Vol. 4, New York: Macmillan.

M.H. Dobb, 1969, *Welfare Economics and the Economics of Socialism*, Cambridge: CUP.

M.H. Dobb, 1970, *Socialist Planning: Some Problems*, London: Lawrence & Wishart.

M.H. Dobb, 1973, *Theories of Value and Distribution since Adam Smith*, Cambridge: CUP.

M.H. Dobb, 1976A, 'A Note on the Ricardo-Marx Discussion', *Science and Society*, Vol. 34.

M.H. Dobb, 1976B, 'Planning', English manuscript as translated for *Enciclopedia Italiana*, Rome: Garzanti.

M.H. Dobb, 1976C, 'Commodity-Production under Socialism', *Socialist Europe*, Vol. 1.

M.H. Dobb, 1978, 'Random Biographical Notes', *Cambridge Journal of Economics*, Vol. 2, No. 2.

R.P. Dutt, 1932, *Communist Review*, September.

A. Erlich, 1960, *The Soviet Industrialisation Debate, 1924-28*, Boston: Harvard UP.

M. Gorbachev, 1987, *Perestroika – New Thinking for our Country and the World*, London: Collins.

A.O. Hirschman, 1958, *The Strategy of Economic Development*, New Haven: Yale UP.

E.J. Hobsbawm, 1967, 'Maurice Dobb', in C. Feinstein (ed.), *Socialism, Capitalism and Economic Growth*, Cambridge: CUP.

E.J. Hobsbawm, 1986, '1956', *Marxism Today*, Vol. 30, No. 10, November.

M. Kalecki, 1968, 'The Marxian Equations of Reproduction and Modern Economics', *Social Science Information*, VII-6, December, Paris, ISSC.

J.M. Keynes, 1925, 'A Short View of Russia', *The Nation and Atheneum*, 1, 17 and 25 October. Reprinted in *Essays in Persuasion* (1931), London: Hart-Davis.

J.M. Keynes, 1930, 'The Question of High Wages', *The Political Quarterly*, January.

J.M. Keynes, 1933, *Essays in Biography*, London: Macmillan.

T. Kowalik, 1964, 'Biography of Michal Kalecki', *Problems of Economic Dynamics and Planning*, Warsaw: PWN.

S. Macintyre, 1980, *A Proletarian Science – Marxism in Britain 1917-1933*, Cambridge: CUP.

K. Marx, 1876, *Critique of the Gotha Programme*, translated in Marx and Engels, 1950, *Selected Works*, Vol. II, London.

B.J. McFarlane and B.H. Pollitt, 1992, 'Maurice Herbert Dobb', in P. Arestis and M. Sawyer (eds.), *A Biographical Dictionary of Dissenting Economists*, Aldershot: Edward Elgar.

B.H. Pollitt, 1988, 'Dobb and Sraffa's Ricardo', *Cambridge Journal of Economics*, Vol. 12, No. 2.

E. Preobrazhensky, 1965, *The New Economics*, translated by Brian Pearce, Oxford: Clarendon Press.

J.V. Robinson, 1964, 'Kalecki and Keynes', *Problems of Economic Dynamics and Planning*, Warsaw: PWN.

W.W. Rostow, 1960, *Stages of Economic Growth*, Cambridge: CUP.

N. Spulber (ed.), 1964, *Foundations of Soviet Economic Growth*, Bloomington: Indiana UP.

P. Sraffa, with the collaboration of M.H. Dobb (ed.), 1951-73, *Works and Correspondence of David Ricardo*, 11 Vols., Cambridge: CUP.

P. Sraffa, 1960, *Production of Commodities by Means of Commodities*, Cambridge: CUP.

L. Szamuely, 1974, *First Models of the Socialist Economic System. Principles and Theories*, Budapest: Central Books (distributors).

Socialist thought

In the half-century prior to the Russian Revolution of 1917 the dominant doctrine inspiring the major socialist parties of continental Europe was Marxism (or was directly derived from Marxism). Since 1917 Marxism has become the official doctrine of the socialist sector of the world (i.e. of the Soviet Union and China and of the other countries of Europe and Asia associated with them). Treated historically, therefore, description and analysis of socialist thought must run predominantly in terms of Marxian doctrine. This is not to say that there have been no other different and rival socialist creeds that have been influential and continue to find an echo today. Marx spoke of the so-called 'Utopian socialists' who had preceded him and in contrast with whom he called his own doctrine 'scientific socialism'. Merging with these, there have been various brands of 'ethical socialists' including the Christian socialists, basing themselves on this or that ethical principle as the pre-eminent one such as 'equality' or 'community values' and on social motives, as against pursuit of 'selfish' individual values and motives. Still others, such as the Fabians in England and the so-called *Kathedersozialisten* and their imitators on the Continent, advocated purely on grounds of expediency an extension of the economic functions and responsibilities of the state, thus identifying their 'socialism' (and its consequential critique of individualism) with *étatisme*. Before coming to Marxism as a social philosophy something must accordingly be said about the historical origins and the varieties of these non-Marxian theories.

UTOPIAN SOCIALISM

The author of one work on the socialist tradition, Sir Alexander Gray, starts with Moses, Lycurgus, and Plato, passing from them to the Essenes and the early Christian Fathers and thence to St.

Thomas Aquinas and Sir Thomas More. Indeed, Plato and More have been cited as forerunners in many a work on the subject. But this article will not go so far back as this. It must be sufficient to distinguish those writers of the eighteenth or early nineteenth century who, in the shadows of the emerging modern world, sought to paint a picture of a perfect society of the future deducible from first principles either of rationality or of morality and attainable only if mankind were sufficiently reasonable or good. Among these was Mably, a French contemporary of Adam Smith, who in a series of quasi-Platonic dialogues developed a critique of the institution of private property and who believed that nature had destined all men to be equal. He argued that the institution of private property both annihilates the primitive and natural equality of man and enables the indolent and unworthy to live at the expense of the active and industrious. Another eighteenth-century figure who both attacked the irrationality of existing society and went into considerable detail about the structure of an ideal society was Morelly (*Code de la nature* 1755).

The most quoted and influential of the architects of a Utopian future were Saint-Simon and Fourier. The former, a count descended from an old and honoured family who renounced his title during the French Revolution, became the founder of something of a school (which included the positivist philosopher Auguste Comte). After his death there was even established a Saint-Simonian church. Among other proposals for the reorganisation of society on new principles he propounded a scheme for productive associations and a *projet de travaux* under the aegis of government and advocated the principle that the rights of property ought to be rooted solely in its contribution to the production of social wealth. Here his disciples, who developed his doctrines in notable respects, went further and preached *the end of* inheritance of property and its eventual transfer to the state. It was they who, incidentally, coined the formula 'from each according to his ability, to each according to his needs'. In his final work, *Nouveau christianisme*, 1825, Saint-Simon sought to expound a new religion dedicated to 'the great aim of the most rapid improvement in the lot of the poorest class ... the most numerous class'. Persecuted and divided, the Saint-Simonian school disintegrated in the course of the 1830s.

Fourier is best known as the author of a scheme for the organisation of *phalansteres*, communities in which both production and social life were to be organised on a cooperative or communal basis. This would allow the natural, inborn 'harmony' of man to be realised – a harmony that existing commercial civilisation had destroyed. In this new society work, instead of being a burden, would be enjoyed.

Another sketch of a communist Utopia was Cabet's *Voyage en Icarie* of 1838. A more direct influence on French socialism in the middle and later nineteenth century was Proudhon, author of *Qu'est-ce que la propriété?*, 1840, and coiner of the aphorism 'Property is theft'. This aphorism was for him the answer to the Lockean right to property by labour. Yet, regarding property, he could be called a 'distributivist' as much as, or even more than a socialist. His influence has been more in the direction of anarchism than of socialism, since two of his central ideas were equality and individual freedom and he preached against communism and the authoritarian state. His remedy for the evil of taking (and living on) interest was a system of universal and interest-free credit to be organised through a mutual credit bank (his system of *mutualité)* – a proposal that not surprisingly drew the fire of Marx's criticism in the latter's *Misère de la philosophie* (See the biographies of Fourier, Proudhon, Saint-Simon).

THE RICARDIAN SOCIALISTS IN ENGLAND

The germ of socialist ideas in England before Marx lay in a critique of classical political economy by a group of writers and pamphleteers who have come to be loosely described as the Ricardian socialists. A centrepiece of this critique for the main figures of this group was a concept of exploitation couched in traditional eighteenth-century terms of 'natural right'. They were Ricardian in the sense that they sought to use Ricardo's theory of value in such a way as to turn it, with the aid of natural-right notions, against the main precepts of the Ricardian school.

By the end of the eighteenth century Spence and Ogilvie had derived from the principle of natural right the conclusion that ownership of land should be shared equally and that no man should have more than he could cultivate. Nature or God had given the land 'in common to all men', and equal sharing of land by all was the basic guarantee and *sine qua non* of human freedom. By analogy, in the year after Ricardo's death William Thompson (in *An Inquiry Into the Principles of the Distribution of Wealth* 1824) deduced the right of labour to the whole produce of labour from the postulate that labour is the sole (active) creator of wealth. In existing society this was prevented by a system of 'unequal exchanges' that resulted in part of labour's product being filched by the possessors of economic advantage. Apart from its injustice and its offence against the Benthamite maxim of 'greatest happiness', this system deprived labour of much of its necessary incentive (substituting want as the spur to labour) and hence was inimical to national wealth. Such a notion could be held to have been implicit to some extent in Adam Smith's treatment of profit and rent as 'deductions' and Ricardo's treatment of them as alternative and rival forms of surplus. But in Thompson's notion of appropriation, or exploitation, what was implicit in his forebears is given an explicit extension that those forebears would probably have disowned. Thompson, incidentally, also attempted a reply to Malthusian pessimism by stressing the historical relativity of population trends.

The year following Thompson's *Inquiry* there appeared Thomas Hodgkin's *Labour Defended against the Claims of Capital*, which opens with the statement, 'Throughout this country at present there exists a serious contest between capital and labour'. (Two years later his lectures at the London Mechanics Institution were published as *Popular Political Economy*). Hodgkin similarly distinguished property associated with one's own labour, which is a natural right, from property as the power to appropriate the product of the labour of others – that is, Lockean 'natural right' from the 'legal or artificial' right of ownership by conquest or appropriation. In a famous passage he declares: 'I am certain that till the triumph of labour be complete; till productive industry alone be opulent, and till idleness alone be poor ... till the right of property shall be founded on principles of justice and not those of slavery ... there cannot and there ought not to be either peace on earth or goodwill amongst men'. Halévy says of his ideas that, while they 'have their starting point in the philosophy of Bentham, it is in the philosophy of Karl Marx that they find their resting place'. Contemporaneously with Hodgkin, in 1825, John Gray published his *Lecture on Human Happiness*. Fourteen years later there appeared J. F. Bray's *Labour's Wrongs and Labour's Remedy*, which also contrasts 'unequal exchanges' with equal and speaks of the exchange between capital and labour as 'legalised robbery'. Both writers ended by advocating somewhat vaguely a kind of Owenite cooperation.

These writers apparently had in common the *a priori* derivation of ideal precepts for rebuilding society from postulated first principles of 'justice' or of 'natural right'. But what links them as forerunners of Marx is their common championship of productive labour against the appropriation of labour's product over and above a subsistence wage, in consequence of the concentration of property ownership in comparatively few hands.

Apart from the French Utopians and English Ricardians, the German economic writer Rodbertus is sometimes included in the category of pre-Marxian socialists and, with his generalised concept of rent, has been called an anticipator of Marx's theory of surplus value. Certainly his theory at first sight has a good deal in common with that of the English Ricardian socialists. But the main concern of his theory was to provide an explanation of crises of overproduction (in terms of underconsumption) and of how these could be prevented. His critique of existing society must be classed as 'conservative socialism', and the social reforms he advocated as a forerunner of 'Bismarckian socialism' rather than of the popular socialist movement as we know it. Again Lassalle (in some respects influenced by Rodbertus) was a populariser and propagandist of socialist ideas rather than a theorist in his own right.

THE FABIANS AND GUILD SOCIALISM

By the end of the century, when Fabian socialism arose in England as a rival both of nineteenth-century economic liberalism and of Marxism, the climate of thinking had changed. Gone was the influence of eighteenth-century rationalism and of the metaphysic of natural right, and gone with them was the habit of deriving ideal models for a future society from some mythical 'natural' state of society in the past. The end of the Victorian era, the time of transition from the age of steam to that of electricity and from free trade to imperialism, had a more practical, more mundane, and more circumscribed cast of thought. The Fabians were not alone in their preoccupation with the inadequacies of laissez-faire and the propriety of extending the economic functions of the state. Certain academic economists, notably Sidgwick, had already opened this question, as earlier Jevons himself had done much more cautiously and as afterward Marshall and his disciple and successor Pigou were to do.

Among the authors of the *Fabian Essays* of 1889 were some famous names, such as Bernard Shaw, Sidney Webb, Graham Wallas, and Sidney Olivier, who, although sharing a common platform, spoke each with an individual accent. Bernard Shaw had been weaned from Marxism to the economic theories of Jevons (under the economist Wicksteed's influence) and from early revolutionary faith to a belief in evolutionary 'gradualism' which was the hallmark of the group as a whole. Webb was the patient empiricist, versed in the literature of royal commissions and acts of Parliament, who could report voluminously and in detail on social ills and inefficiencies needing remedy and the practical steps by which governmental action could remove them. In his Fabian essay he remarks that 'history shews us no example of the sudden substitution of Utopian and revolutionary romance', attacks the age of individualism as the age of anarchy, and advances a radical programme of specific reforms as the necessary complement to political democracy. As a group, the Fabians were concerned with particular evils and remedial measures, rather than with any general philosophy of society or even (Shaw excepted) with the denunciation of private property and the receipt of rent, interest, and profit. Much emphasis was laid on efficiency, and their essential method would probably be called today 'social engineering'. Some have even denied them the name 'socialists', owing to their lack of interest in any radical reconstitution of the property basis of society. Perhaps it is in Bernard Shaw, and in him only, that are found traces of continuity with earlier brands of socialism, whether of the English or the Continental variety, since he makes polemical use (in the *Fabian Essays* and in others of his works) of a generalised concept of rent as 'unearned surplus' reminiscent of Marxian surplus value – a socially created surplus, which ought to be appropriated by society and not by individuals.

Close on the heels of the Fabians – and to a large extent as a reaction against the strong element of *étatisme* in their outlook – came the comparatively short-lived but luminous movement known as 'guild socialism'. Originating in a group of writers connected with the journal *New Age* (edited by A.R. Orage) in the first decade of the present century, it was soon reinforced by recruits from the contemporary university generation (mainly Oxford Fabians and most notably G.D.H. Cole). It drew largely upon the ideas of the French syndicalists, with their emphasis on industrial direct action and the 'industrial democracy' of direct workers' control, to correct the centralising and bureaucratising bias traditional to state socialism. (Cole's early work, *The World of Labour* of 1913, is eloquent of this French inspiration.) Their target of attack was less the particular inefficiencies of capitalist individualism than the evils and the hateful human degradation of 'wage slavery', with labour treated as a commodity, the abolition of which required that the social ownership of industrial capital be combined with the organisation of industry under the control of democratic guilds composed of the actual producers (i.e., workers by hand and brain in the industries in question). Industrial democracy in this form was necessary not only to emancipate the workers but also to complement, indeed to realise, political democracy. In their theory of the state, guild socialists tended to be pluralist and to reject the notion of state sovereignty. In its denunciation of wage slavery guild socialism had more affinity with earlier and with Continental socialist thought than had the more insular English Fabianism.

MARXIAN SOCIALISM

Not surprisingly, in view of its Hegelian roots, Marxian socialism started with a philosophy of history and a methodology. In a much-quoted phrase, Marx spoke of finding Hegel standing on his head and of proceeding to set him on his feet. This he claimed to have done by enunciating his materialist interpretation of history. According to this, it was the mode of production of any given epoch that was the key to the interpretation of that epoch, including its 'superstructure' of ideas and moral sentiments and its legal and political institutions. This 'mode of production' was conceived of as embracing not only its productive technology but also the prevailing 'social relations of production' – namely, relations between men which turned upon their relations to the process of production and in particular to ownership of the means of production. In effect, these were class relations, and the contradictions inherent in such relations were the basis of class struggle, the prime mover of historical change to date.

History since the end of tribal society had witnessed three main modes of production: slavery, feudal serfdom, and modern capitalism based on wage labour. All of these were forms of class society – each marked by class antagonism in its specific way – in which the producer was in a position of subjection to a ruling class whose power rested on ownership. In consequence of this subjection the surplus product, over and above what the producer himself retained for subsistence, was appropriated by the ruling and owning class, whether slaveowners, feudal *seigneurs*, or capitalists. In the first of these socioeconomic forms, the ruling class owned the person of the labouring producer as well as the impersonal, material means of production. In the second, it had the legal right to annex a certain portion of the labour time of the producer, whether in the form of direct labour services or of tribute in kind. In the third, the labourer was in legal status a free agent, the relation between him and the capitalist being that of a contractual market relationship, yet the economic compulsion of his propertyless status obliged the proletarian wage earner to sell his labour power for little more than a subsistence wage (or for even less in conditions of acute unemployment). Thus the Wage-Labour-Capital relationship under capitalism bore a major analogy with earlier and more patently servile forms of class relationship; and property right per se was able to draw to its possessor, independently of any productive activity, a share of the total product.

This, in brief, was Marx's concept of exploitation (and as fruit of exploitation, class struggle). His economic analysis, as expounded in *Das Kapital*, was designed to enlarge on this analogy with previous modes of appropriating surplus product and to show how the persistence of a difference between the value of labour power (sold for wages) and the value of its product was consistent with the 'law of value'– that is, with conditions of a free market and of perfect competition. Unlike earlier socialist writers, he did not deduce the existence of surplus value or exploitation from some principle of natural right of labour to its product (all too often supposed by commentators and critics to be inherent in the labour theory of value). The analogy with earlier modes of appropriating a surplus product was for him a historical datum, which he sought to explain in terms of economic theory – doing so by penetrating below the market 'appearance' of things to the 'essence' of social relations under capitalism (the relationship between capitalist and proletarian as that of owner and propertyless). For this reason, the boundaries of economic analysis were drawn more widely than in the narrower market-equilibrium studies to which we have grown accustomed in post-Menger, post-Jevonian economics, from which property relations and their influence are excluded because they are thought to belong to social rather than to economic theory.

Marx's explanation turned on his distinction, to which he attached great importance, between labour and labour power. Labour power was what was sold as a commodity in return for wages and, like other commodities, sold for a price determined by the cost in labour necessary to produce and reproduce it. This was the cost of producing its own subsistence – its essential input (this being modified, as Marx like Ricardo, allowed, by an historically relative factor of social habit and custom). Hence wages absorbed only *part* of the product of labour at work for any given length of time – the value of labour power as a productive input was never more than a fraction of the net output emerging from the productive process. The difference was surplus-value, which accrued to title of ownership as profit, interest, or rent.

In this consisted the main part of his critical diagnosis of contemporary society. But it was also fundamental to his prediction of the dynamic of capitalist society and his prediction of its eventual replacement by socialism. With the development of the capitalist mode of production the class struggle would develop both in extent and in acuteness. With the widening and deepening of exploitation the proletariat would acquire class consciousness and would develop its own organisation, both economic and political, as the eventual instrument of capital's overthrow. But there were two other agents of the dynamic process. First, there was a continuous tendency both toward concentration of production into larger units and toward centralisation of capital itself, tendencies that at the same time encouraged more concentrated and more enduring organisation of labour, while confronting labour with a more centralised, impersonal, and tyrannical foe. Second, because of its uncoordinated character (its characteristic 'anarchy of production'), combined with a growing contradiction between the rates of growth of the enlargement of productive power and the enlargement of growth of markets, the process of capital accumulation was periodically interrupted by dislocating economic crises of overproduction. Such crises served the function of re-creating the reserve army of the unemployed when it became depleted by the expanding demand for labour and wages showed signs of rising and encroaching upon surplus-value. They also encouraged the tendency to concentration on the side of capital (the larger swallowing the smaller in lean years) and increased the instability of the worker's status and condition.

The inevitable outcome and only 'solution' to these gathering contradictions was a revolt of organised labour against the growing tyranny of capital, as the latter showed itself increasingly to be a 'fetter on production', no longer revolutionising technique and expanding productive capacity as it had done in its halcyon days but restricting and wasting productive capacity and holding it in check. On its negative side such a revolt could only take the form of dispossessing the capitalists of their ownership rights – the famous 'expropriation of the expropriators'. On its positive side revolutionary transformation must take the form of the transfer of the means of production into social ownership and the social organisation of production on a planned basis, since in conditions of modern technique and large-scale industrial production the kind of solution favoured by Saint-Simon and Proudhon – the distribution of property in small units to all citizens – was clearly impracticable.

A social transformation of this kind, the most revolutionary known to history, would liquidate the class antagonism of previous class society by substituting the social equality of a community of active producers, where everyone was a worker drawing an income from society, for the unequal and divided society of those who owned and those who were dispossessed. The period of human history characterised by successive forms of class exploitation, each with its specific type of dominant and exploiting class appropriating surplus product in its own manner, would have closed. But this did not mean that historical change would have come to an end. The technical means of production would continue to develop, probably more rapidly than before; human organisation, in adaptation to changing economic conditions and needs, would perennially undergo change. But the basic cause of social antagonism as known before in human history would have disappeared.

There was no pretence, however, that the relative social equality of all citizens as workers and producers would be the realisation of an ideal of absolute justice among men. Socialists of the Marxian school have always spoken (since Marx wrote his *Critique of the Gotha Programme*) of two stages of socialism, a lower and a higher. In the former although work incomes would constitute the sole category of income, and inequalities due to the existence of property incomes would have disappeared, some differences of income would still remain owing to the necessity of differentiating wages according to the amount and kind of work performed. Only at the latter stage, when the productive powers of society had been sufficiently developed and the moral standards of society sufficiently raised, would it be possible to achieve the fuller social equality of 'from each according to his ability, to each according to his needs'. It has become customary in recent decades to call the first 'socialism' and to reserve the name of 'communism' for the second. One could say that the former would realise equality of opportunity for all, but the effect upon individual incomes of inequality of human capacities and talents would not be eliminated; only under 'full communism' would differences of human capacities and needs cease to be of economic significance.

Marx and Engels and their followers always regarded it as inconsistent with their conception and method to prepare anything resembling a blueprint of the future socialist society. The attempt to do so was the hallmark of the Utopian socialist, and in their ascetic refusal to emulate their predecessors in this respect, they stood at the opposite pole from Fourier and his obsessive love of detailed prescription. Socialism, it was stated, would be established by 'the proletariat organised as the ruling class', which would forthwith 'convert the means of production into State property'; it would 'centralise all elements of production in the hands of the State' (i.e., of the proletariat organised as the ruling class) and would 'increase the total of productive powers as rapidly as possible'. There were some occasional hints in the writings of Marx and Engels that production would be organised consciously under some kind of prearranged social plan. But apart from the comments already quoted from the *Critique of the*

Gotha Programme, that is virtually all. Lenin, who had the task of laying the foundations of the first socialist state, declared that 'in Marx there is no trace of attempts to create Utopias, to guess in the void at what cannot be known'.

POST-1917 SOCIAL DEMOCRACY

In the years since the Russian Revolution the socialist world has been more or less sharply divided between those who recognised this event as a genuine socialist revolution and those who denied it such a name. The difference partly turned on the methods used to achieve and consolidate the revolution, namely the use of insurrection and armed force and the regime of the 'dictatorship of the proletariat'. But there was also the deeper issue of whether socialism could be built at all in a backward country of weakly developed industry and predominantly peasant agriculture. The Russian Mensheviks denied that it could be and declared that the stage was set in Russia for no more than a 'bourgeois revolution' against tsarist absolutism. What was distinctively new in Lenin's controversial interpretation when he arrived back in Russia in April 1917 was that, while accepting that a bourgeois revolution was in process, he nonetheless declared that the industrial proletariat could and should seize power in alliance with the peasantry and in doing so could transform a bourgeois revolution into a socialist one and in the fullness of time start to build socialism. The discussion about 'socialism in one country' that was to develop within the Bolshevik ranks in the following decade was in large degree an extension of this same controversy, since it was concerned with the question of whether the transition to socialism, already started by the nationalisation decrees of 1917-1918 and carried over into the 'mixed economy' of the 1920s, could be *completed* unless the revolution spread to other, more technically advanced, countries of Europe.

Socialist parties in Western Europe (with the exception of the Italian) generally followed the Menshevik line in their estimate of the Soviet revolution. They proceeded to affirm their devotion to democratic parliamentary methods and their intention of achieving socialism, not by a single revolutionary act, but by a series of modifying reforms in the existing structure and by a gradual extension of the economic functions of government. The rift in socialist thought and policy was deepened after the formation of the Third (or Communist) International in 1919 in opposition to the Second International, which after its collapse in 1914 was to be revived in 1920. The concept of socialism current in most social democratic circles increasingly approached that of Fabian gradualism and in the course of two decades, in most cases ceased to be Marxian in anything but name. After World War II, partly under pressure of the 'Cold War', the leading parties of continental Europe and Scandinavia not only eschewed Marxism, but dropped from their programmes any proposal for extensive socialisation of production.

Some would say that the temper of the times is to eschew general social theories as speculative or metaphysical and that for this reason one can no longer speak of socialist theory apart from the Marxist school. Certainly it is true that the tendency in England and elsewhere has been to favour an increasingly empirical approach. Sixty-three years after the appearance of the original *Fabian Essays* a number of younger thinkers of the British Labour party combined to produce in 1952 a collection of *New Fabian Essays* under the editorship of R.H.S. Crossman. What is remarkable about this new volume, in contrast with the emphasis of its forebear, is the playing down of socialisation in the traditional sense of the transfer of means of production to state ownership (even to the point of dismissing it as an obsolete Marxian prejudice). If there is a single unifying theme in terms of which socialism as a credo is here definable, it is perhaps to be found in an emphasis on social equality. This is to be realised primarily through the extension of social services, a widening of educational opportunities, and progressive taxation. Indeed, one writer, C.A.R. Crosland, speaks as though the aims of the socialist movement were already achieved to a considerable extent, since the metamorphosis of capitalism 'into a quite different system ... is rendering academic most of the traditional socialist analysis', and state intervention in economic life has so increased as to 'justify the statement that the capitalist era has now passed into history'. Property rights, it is said, 'no longer constitute the essential basis of economic and social power', which has passed to a new class of managers. Nationalisation and 'the early Fabian emphasis on collectivism' are expressly rejected as key to the definition of socialism, and equality of status is enthroned as the essence of the definition instead. Before the war, in 1937, Douglas Jay in *The Socialist Case* had already said, 'If we are to have the substance and not the shadow, we must define socialism as the abolition of private unearned or inherited incomes rather than of the private ownership of the means of production'; while as for planning in any of its forms, these are 'possible rather than necessary elements of socialism'.

THE ECONOMISTS' DEBATE

There remains to be said something in summary about the narrower economists' discussion of socialism which itself falls into two halves: discussion of the comparative merits of the two rival systems in the attainment of some postulated 'optimum' and discussion of alternative mechanisms, or 'models', for the operation of a socialist economy. The latter has become a lively subject of debate today in the socialist countries themselves.

As a result of the new economics of Jevons and Menger in the last quarter of the nineteenth century, two opposite tendencies arose among leading academic figures. Firstly, as we have noted, there was a tendency in England especially (which Jevons himself cautiously initiated) to re-examine the case for laissez-faire and the exceptions to it. This re-examination, developed by Sidgwick and Marshall, drew attention to a number of 'exceptions', in which public interest conflicted with private and in which production of wealth failed to be maximised when left to the free play of market forces. In the twentieth century, with the increasing prevalence of monopoly and restricted competition, this critique was extended to include the adverse effects of 'imperfect competition' or 'monopolistic competition' – the excess capacity latent in excessive product differentiation and also the swollen costs and distorting effects of salesmanship and advertising to which they give rise. Secondly, and concurrently, the development of mathematical theories of general market equilibrium brought with it, as a signal corollary, a new justification of free enterprise: namely, that the general equilibrium toward which a competitive market always tends represents a maximum of utility (in given conditions of demand and of economic resources). This corollary of their analysis was underlined by Walras and popularised by his follower Pareto. What made this theorem on inspection less impressive than at first appeared was that the postulated optimum was relative to a given income distribution (or at least of a given structure of factor ownership taken as datum). Hence, it could not be used to pass judgement on income distribution itself. Its critics pointed out that the Walras-Pareto theorem defined, not a unique optimum position, but a whole series of positions. In a modified form, however, the theorem continued to be used as a justification of free competition as that which secures an optimum result *relative* to whatever income distribution existed (it being implicitly recognised that the State could, and should, modify that income distribution through taxation – so far as disincentive effects of taxation upon production allowed).

Soon, however, a counterattack was mounted upon the socialist case with the aid of this theorem, in the form of the contention that a socialist economy, since it would lack a market for factors of production, would have no way of attaining an optimum (of utility or welfare) or even of ascertaining in what direction this lay. Hence, in the words of von Mises (the name chiefly associated with this argument), a socialist economy would be non-rational and uneconomic *ex natura* (1922). In the two decades that followed von Mises's challenge, socialist economists (in Germany in the course of the 1920s and in England and the United States in the 1930s) sought an answer to it by demonstrating various ways in which the problem could be solved. Most of the suggested mechanisms, however, involved the creation of actual markets or else of quasi-market processes for factors of production and 'producers goods' (i.e., all productive inputs) and the simulation of competition under socialism. Henry Dickinson, for example, proposed actual markets; Lange proposed a system of accounting prices to be adjusted so as to equilibrate supply and demand by a trial-and-error process, with output decisions and investment decisions taken on the basis of these accounting prices according to certain rules (1936-1937). Such solutions mainly implied decentralised decision making (at the level of individual industries or enterprises) and accordingly set limits to the amount of centralised planning (other than 'indicative planning') that could be used. This was not the case, however, with all the suggested solutions. In 1908, for example, the Italian economist Barone had already advanced one such solution in mathematical form. But doubt was expressed as to whether, as a centralised planning solution, it could be regarded as practicable in view of the complexity of the calculations involved.

It should be added that the further discussion of what has come to be called 'welfare economics', especially in the course of the 1950s, has introduced considerable doubt as to whether the maximising of welfare or of national output (or income) could be given any precise meaning. In both cases this doubt was primarily due to the aforementioned difficulty of income distribution; in the second case, for example, it was due to the dependence of prices, in terms of which output is summed into an aggregate, upon income distribution. There was the difficulty introduced by a growing emphasis on the conventional element in wants and the influence of other people's consumption on an individual's satisfactions, as well as the effect of advertising propaganda ('the hidden persuaders') upon desires. Even if sense could still be conceded to the idea of maximising something, it followed that the 'tolerances' to be allowed to any mechanism for achieving it were considerably wider than had earlier been supposed.

During the 1950s the question of more, or less, centralised or decentralised models and of the degree to which planning and a market mechanism could be combined also began to occupy economic discussion in the socialist countries of eastern Europe. On the one hand, this discussion was provoked by the need to give more initiative to the individual industrial enterprise in regard to the choice of inputs and outputs (within a general framework of planning) in a period when considerations of efficiency, quality, innovation, and attention to consumers' requirements were becoming more important than mere quantitative increase of output of a given range of products, which had been the main preoccupation of an earlier period. Combined with this was a reconsideration of the type of collective incentive to the enterprise that would be most conducive to the beneficial use of this initiative. On the other hand, the discussion was prompted by an increasing use of linear programming methods for selecting an optimum plan from among a range of alternative and self-consistent plans, according to the system of the Leningrad mathematician Kantorovitch. Such methods of optimal planning can be applied at various levels – that is, to decentralised or centralised decisions, to integral parts of a plan, or to a plan as a larger whole (at the time of writing they have been applied only to the former). In each optimal solution there is implicit a set of 'shadow prices', in terms of which the cost of inputs necessary to yield a given output program is minimised (or alternatively the output yielded by a given quantity of available inputs is maximised). Accordingly, the question of what system of prices is consistent with the choice of optimum methods of production is immediately raised.

The Yugoslav economy was the first socialist economy to adopt a fairly drastic degree of decentralisation, early in the 1950s. This took the form of giving economic enterprises greater discretion in their output programmes (and even in large measure their investments) on the basis of contractual arrangements with other industries, enterprises, or wholesale and retail bodies. Yugoslavia is often cited, accordingly, as an example of a 'decentralised market model'. In recent years, however, other countries, including the Soviet Union, have in varying degrees moved in the direction of decentralisation of planning and of freeing the enterprise as a decision-making unit from a surfeit of detailed directives. New 'models' of decentralised (contractual) supply arrangements and enterprise autonomy linked with collective enterprise incentives have been experimented with especially in consumer goods industries (e.g., the Liberman scheme in the USSR and the Šik proposals in Czechoslovakia).

But while in the socialist countries increased concern has been shown with optimal planning, among Western economists the focus of interest has been shifting away from questions of static equilibria to questions of growth. One could say that most economists are more concerned today to use growth potential as a criterion of judgment for an economic system than to use its capability either for attaining an economically perfect allocation of productive resources (defined in some way) or for ensuring an equitable distribution of income. On the relative weight to be attached to such criteria opinion naturally varies among economists, as it always has done and continues to do among socialists. But so far as a growth criterion is concerned, there can be little doubt that socialist economies have a distinctly good record: *vide* the high rates of growth in Soviet industry in the pre-war decade and again in the planned economies as a whole in the post-war period. (In agriculture, on the other hand, although there have at times been successes, the record is less impressive). Long-term planning in the Soviet Union in particular has set itself the goal of maintaining an industrial growth rate in the neighbourhood of 10 per cent during this and the ensuing decade, and of overtaking the US economy both in absolute production and in per capita production at an early date. Much in the comparative economic judgment of the two systems will no doubt turn on the result.

BIBLIOGRAPHY

Max Beer (1919-1920), 1953, A *History of British Socialism.* 2 vols. London: Allen & Unwin. Based on Beer's *Geschichte des Sozialismus in England*, 1912.

Avram Bergson (1948), 1954, 'Socialist Economics', Volume I, pages 412-448 in Howard S. Ellis (editor), A *Survey of Contemporary Economics.* Homewood, Ill.: Irwin.

Wlodzimierz Bris, 1961, *Ogólne problemy funkcjonowania gospodarki socjalistycznej* (General Problems in the Functioning of a Socialist Economy), Warsaw: Panstwowe Wydawnictwo Naukowe.

Emile Burns, 1935, *A Handbook of Marxism*, London: Gollancz.

Edward H. Carr, 1951-1964, *History of Soviet Russia.* 7 vols. New York: Macmillan. Volumes 1-3: *The Bolshevik Revolution, 1917-1923*, 1951-1953. Volume 4: *The Interregnum, 1923-1924*, 1954. Volumes 5-7: *Socialism in One Country, 1924-1926*, 1958-1964. See especially Volume 1, Chapters 1-2 and Volume 2, Chapter 15.

G.D.H. Cole, 1953-1960, *A History of Socialist Thought.* 5 vols. New York: St. Martins; London: Macmillan. Volume 1: *Socialist Thought: The Forerunners, 1789-1850*, 1953. Volume 2: *Marxism and Anarchism, 1850-1890*, 1954. Volume 3: *The Second International, 1889-1914*, 2 parts, 1956. Volume 4: *Communism and Social Democracy, 1914-1931*, 2 parts, 1958. Volume 5: *Socialism and Fascism, 1931-1939*, 1960.

Henry Dickinson, 1939, *Economics of Socialism,* Oxford Univ. Press.

Alexander Gray, 1946, *The Socialist Tradition: Moses to Lenin.* London: Longmans.

Friedrich A. von Hayek et al., 1935, *Collectivist Economic Planning: Critical Studies on the Possibilities of Socialism*, London: Routledge.

Carl Landauer, 1959, *European Socialism: A History of Ideas and Movements From the Industrial Revolution to Hitler's Seizure of Power.* 2 vols. Berkely: Univ. of California Press. Volume 1: *From the Industrial Revolution to the First World War and Its Aftermath.*

Volume 2: *The Socialist Struggle Against Capitalism and Totalitarianism.*

Oskar Lange (1936-1937), 1952, 'On the Economic Theory of Socialism', pages 55-143, in Benjamin E. Lippincott (editor), *On the Economic Theory of Socialism*, Minneapolis: University of Minnesota Press. First published in Volume 4 of the *Review of Economic Studies.*

George Lichtheim (1961), 1964, *Marxism: An Historical and Critical Study*, 2d ed. Rev. London: Routledge.

Franz Mehring (1918), 1948, *Karl Marx: The Story of His Life*, London: Allen & Unwin. First published in German. A paperback edition was published in 1962 by the Univ. of Michigan Press.

Arthur C. Pigou, 1937, *Socialism Versus Capitalism*, London: Macmillan.

Rudolf Schlesinger, 1950, *Marx: His Time and Ours*, New York: Kelley.

G.M. Steklov (1919), 1928, *History of the First International*, London: Lawrence. Translated from the 3d Russian edition.

Ludwig Von Mises (1922), 1959, *Socialism: An Economic and Sociological Analysis*, New ed., enl. New Haven: Yale Univ. Press. First published as *Die Gemeinwirtschaft.*

The centenary of *Capital* and its relevance today

Marx has sometimes been dubbed 'the last of the classical economists' (meaning by the latter the school of Classical Political Economy: a term coined by Marx himself to describe essentially the system of doctrine built up by Adam Smith and Ricardo which flowered particularly during the first three decades of the 19th century). Whether this description of him is true or false – and there *is* a sense in which it is *not* altogether false or misleading – it remains a fact that it has become fashionable in recent decades to dismiss Marx, along with the whole Classical School as an out-of-date relic of the 19th century, of historical interest perhaps but without any contemporary application to the present century or relevance to Socialist theory and practice today. Not only is this view taught in our seats of learning – or implied by silence and by the fact that no economics student is required to read him – but one finds it pronounced from the platform at Labour Party Conferences. Nevertheless, a certain reaction against this view has been discenible among economists, or at least some of them, during the past ten or 15 years. This is associated with the growing vogue of theories of growth and development, and connected with it a concern with what it is fashionable to call 'macroscopic' problems and relations (by contrast with 'microscopic'): tendencies that have been explicitly recognised by some as being a return to the kind of preoccupation and approach that characterized the Classics, and more especially Marx (for example, his concern with what he called the general 'law of motion' of capitalist society). Also discernible today are less obvious ways in which Marx's approach and emphasis are exerting an influence on non-Marxists, even if this influence is often unrecognized and unacknowledged, indirect or even second hand. Among the young in the Left movement, especially among students, one can say that interest in Marxism is moving sharply upwards once again.

That Marx should have been not only criticized but also misunderstood and distorted is perhaps not altogether surprising, since *Das Kapital* is, I suppose, the most controversial work on Political Economy ever to have been written, and carries its condemnation of the present system on almost every page of Volume I in far from muted language. The subject of more and sharper controversy even than was Ricardo's *Principles* when that work appeared, it has met with wider extremes of praise and denigration, probably, than any other work of its kind. More frequently 'refuted' than most economic theories, it has survived, not only to witness the social revolution that it forecast, but to be accepted over a large part of the contemporary world as the authoritative interpretation of capitalist society. (Even in the final decade of the 19th century his leading critic – Böhm-Bawerk – could complain that 'Marx has become the apostle of a wide circle of readers, including many who are not as a rule given to the reading of difficult books'). Nearer to our own day, Joseph Schumpeter, with remarkable objectivity, has said of Marx (in his monumental *History of Economic Analysis*) that 'the totality of his vision, as a totality, asserts its right in every detail and is precisely the source of the intellectual fascination experienced by everyone, friend as well as foe, who makes a study of him'; adding that 'at the time when his first volume appeared, there was nobody in Germany who could have measured himself against him either in vigour of thought or in theoretical knowledge'.

Undoubtedly the two features of Marx's work that have been the most controversial, as well as central to his doctrinal system and most striking in their novelty, are his theory of surplus-value (or property-income as the fruit of exploitation) and his theory of the historical development of capitalist society, through and by its quintessential contradictions, towards revolutionary transformation into socialism; the crucial agency of this transformation being the organised working class. Both of these conceptions, moreover, illustrate very fully the extent to which, and the sense in which, his economic analysis of capitalist production is *historical* in character, and an application of 'historical materialism' to a particular socio-economic form. (One might ask the sceptics, including the

Leader of the Labour Party, how could such an analysis *fail* to be of major relevance to socialist theory and practice today? Is there much doubt of the answer if one asked any Trade Union shop steward whether the notion of exploitation and of class conflict had ceased to have application to industry today?).

I need hardly remind you that Marx's doctrine of Historical Materialism treated human history since the end of tribal society as essentially a succession of modes of production, each characterized by a specific structure of what he termed 'social relations of production' (or class relations), hinging on the relation in which various social groups stood to the productive process and to ownership of the basic means of production. The crucial motive force of change consisted of contradictions within this mode of production between the productive forces and productive relations, reflected as regards the latter in class antagonism or class struggle.

All these preceding social forms had been essentially systems of exploitation, in the sense that the surplus product over and above the subsistence of the direct producer was annexed by a ruling class of overlords by dint of political or legal right or compulsion. And at various times and at various places Marx paid a considerable amount of attention to 'pre-capitalist economic formations'. The crucial issue confronting Marx regarding the capitalist mode of production was: how could its obvious analogy as a system of exploitation with those previous forms of class society be squared with the rule of competition and of the market as epitomized in the classical economists' law of value? The latter had, indeed, denied (at least by implication) that there could be any such thing as 'appropriation' or 'exploitation' under capitalism, because on a competitive market everything was ruled by free contract and exchange tended always to take place at value-equivalents (an idea that in various guises is still current today). If there were any such thing as exploitation, then the remedy was freer trade and more competition. This was the problem that Marx, with his concept of surplus-value, set out to solve. The answer (as you doubtless know) turned on the historical creation of a proletariat, deprived of access to the means of production, thus creating a situation where labour-power came upon the market as a commodity (sold for what it 'cost' to reproduce, namely its subsistence). In an oft-quoted passage in Vol. I Marx said: 'The historical conditions of its [Capital's] existence is by no means given with the mere circulation of money and commodities. It can spring into life only when the owner of the means of production and subsistence meets in the market with the free labourer selling his labour-power' (Vol. I, p148). To this he adds: 'This one historical condition comprises a world's history. Capital, therefore, announces from its first appearance a new epoch in the process of social production'. In this way a *difference* between the value of labour-power and of its product appeared – indeed became a 'normal' and unnoticed feature of the economic horizon. And it followed, naturally, that exploitation could only be ended by abolishing the capitalist wage-system.

It is true, of course, that Marx's 'surplus-value' could be regarded as a development of what is a hint (no more than a hint) of a 'deduction theory' of profit to be found in Adam Smith; also of Ricardo's notion of rent of land as a surplus ('not a new creation of revenue, but a transfer of revenue already created'). It is also true that the notion of the exploitation of Labour by Capital had been a theme of that group of writers like Thomas Hodgkin to whom the name of 'Ricardian Socialists' has subsequently been given. But none of these ever posed the issue squarely in the way that Marx did (and as I've just described it). What made his theory of surplus value unique was that he showed that it could be reconciled with the classical theory of value – indeed, written in terms of it; and hence be demonstrated as perfectly consistent with the vaunted rule of competition and the sovereignty of the 'free market'.

To come to his second, and closely related, concept of the historical development of capitalism as an economic system: development through growing concentration of capital, sharpening of crises and class antagonism until capitalist relations of production came to be clearly seen as a fetter upon the system's own developing productive forces. Certainly, many of the classical writers had also shown concern with the future possibilities of capital accumulation, and were obsessed by the possible threat of a halting of progress in a so-called 'stationary state' (what today would be spoken of as a 'stagnationist tendency'). But in its Ricardian form the threat (of rising rents and falling profits, as he saw it) only held if corn-input continued to be restricted and foreign trade was not free. So far as the process of capital accumulation itself and the system of industry were concerned, there was no internal flaw, no danger of breakdown: given only free import and free trade to keep food cheap and hence labour-power, capitalist development could proceed smoothly, without serious let or hindrance, until the millennium, with all classes (save possibly landlords) sharing in the benefits of economic progress. Again, the unique contribution of Marx was to show the historical limits to Capitalism as an historic system as set by its own *internal mechanism* or structure, as a system of production – by the contradictions (substantially *class* contradictions) that were of its very nature as a system of exploitation. As Lenin was to put it: 'The study of the productive relationships in a given, historically determinate society, in their genesis, their development and their decay – such was the essential content of Marx's economic teaching'.

At this point it is perhaps appropriate to deal with a not-unimportant misunderstanding about the relation between Marx's theory of value and his concept of surplus-value – a misunderstanding that has been fairly common not only among his critics but also among disciples. This is the idea that the existence of surplus-value and the fact that Labour is exploited are somehow *derived* from the Labour Theory of Value (in the sense of the postulate that things exchange in proportion to the quantity of labour embodied in them) – derived, i.e. in the sense in which the consequent of a syllogism is derived from premiss. This would make it some kind of successor to John Locke's theory of 'natural right' – the natural right of a man to the produce of his own labour (the kind of interpretation given, incidentally, in an interesting study by Professor Richard Schlatter called *Private Property: History of an Idea*). I believe this is mistaken, because semi-idealistic 'natural right' notions were alien to Marx's thought: Marx was not concerned with composing an ethical or moral treatise on exploitation, but a scientific-economic analysis of its nature and its roots; and he himself describes the problem (in *Value, Price and Profit*) as being how to *reconcile* surplus value with exchange according to values, and in a letter to Engels hails discovery of the distinction between labour and labour-power as being crucial to such an explanation. (The passage in *Value, Price and Profit* to which I refer is the one which you may remember where he says: 'To explain the general nature of profits, you have to start from the theorem that on an average commodities are sold at their real values ... If you cannot explain profit upon this supposition, you cannot explain it at all'.).

Does this, then, mean that his theory of value is purely incidental – that the reason for his choosing *this* particular theory was essentially historical, and that any other value theory would have served equally well? No – this, I believe, would also be a misunderstanding, as it were of an opposite kind. As I see it (and have expressed it more than once before) his adoption of what was essentially the classical theory of value (in its Ricardian form at least) was because he saw this as an embodiment of the truth (a truth, again, central to his *historical* interpretation) that in the final analysis conditions of production determined conditions of exchange – for any fundamental explanation and understanding of phenomena visible to the eye on the surface of the market one had to look deeper into the relations of production beneath. Implied in it one could also say – or rather implied in the dual aspect of labour and labour-power as the unique form of productive activity to which the role of the non-human forces of production ('objects' and 'instruments' of labour) are in a significant sense *subordinate*. (One very obvious implication of the latter being that one cannot attribute the operations of such inanimate objects and instruments to their *owners* as a productive activity of the latter – as the sophistries of bourgeois political economy have often sought to do).

Do I need to add that, of course, his theory did *not* amount to a proposition that things necessarily and everywhere exchanged in proportion to embodied labour? This is plain vulgarization – and there is a 'vulgar Marxism' as well as 'vulgar bourgeois political economy'. Under certain (simplified) conditions they would do so. But there were refracting and modifying influences within the sphere of circulation or exchange; and as we well know from his theory of so-called Prices of Production in Volume III, the requirement of an equal profit-rate on capital (a requirement enforced by the competition and mobility of capitals) obliges exchange-ratios to diverge from Value to the extent that compositions of capital vary as between different industries. Further, of course, short-period market-price (or again monopoly-price) may diverge, in turn, from Prices of Production. All this is *part* of Marx's theory of value in its full dimensions, unvulgarised.

Compounding (as Americans would say) one misunderstanding with another, his critics at this point have thrown down the following challenge. If, then, as turns out in Volume III of *Capital*, commodities exchange after all, *not* at their values, but at prices of production, which diverge from labour-values, what is left of the theory of surplus-value? If we are to believe what is said in Volume III, what is left standing of Volume I? To turn Marx in this way against himself was the method used (as you no doubt know) by his most influential critic, the Austrian von Böhm-Bawerk (both a Professor and Finance Minister in Imperial Vienna), at the end of the 19th century in his polemical work *Zum Abschluss des Marxschen System* (Close of the Marxian System); with its central thesis of 'The Great Contradiction' on which it was claimed that the whole theory of surplus-value and class conflict foundered. 'The Marxian system', it was confidently proclaimed, 'has a past and present, but no abiding future'. The point is (which Böhm-Bawerk and his imitators failed to see) that prices of production, while diverging from values, bore a definite or determinate relation to them: in a logical and quantitative sense the former could be 'derived' from the latter (and from other conditions of production, such as technical conditions governing the composition of capitals), which was the warp and weft of Volume I. In particular they rested on the postulation of a certain rate of exploitation as defined in value-terms; and the theory of Volume III was by no means left hanging in the air, lacking a pediment or base in conditions of production and exploitation – as it *would* have been, of course, in the absence of the theory of value and surplus-value of Volume I.

What remains true is that the precise way in which Marx in Volume III derives Prices of Production from Values is defective, and in the form in which it is there expressed will not stand up. There is, indeed, a passage in his *Theorien über den Mehrwert* where Marx shows himself aware of this deficiency. (As we know from Engels' Preface, the manuscript for Volume III was left unfinished as well as in places rough and incomplete on Marx's death). Put as briefly as I can, the point is that *only* the outputs, and not the inputs, were transformed from values into terms of prices of production. For a complete demonstration or solution, it is obvious that *both* must be so transformed. If the prices of so-called wage-goods or of machines diverge from values, then obviously the variable capital and constant capital entering into production as inputs must also be equivalently affected and transformed (or re-priced). Accordingly *ratios* like the rate of surplus-value and rate of profit may also differ in their price-expression from their value-expression: one cannot assume that they will remain the same. This does not mean, however, that a determinate relation between the two cannot be demonstrated – that Marx's claim was wrong that 'values stand behind prices of production' and 'determine these latter in the last resort'. It means simply that the demonstration has to take the more complex form of the solution of a set of simultaneous equations.

I don't wish to let this lecture get bogged down in technicalities, of interest only to economic specialists; and what has come to be know as the 'Transformation Problem' (i.e. transforming Values into Prices) can be said to be of mainly formal interest – if nonetheless quite crucial for the logical structure of the Marxian system. Let me only say this. Discussion of this problem over the past half-century (to which, regrettably, orthodox Marxists have contributed all-too-little, even when they have been aware of the problem) has established that such a solution and such a demonstration are quite possible. The pioneer effort in this direction was that of Bortkievicz exactly sixty years ago, showing that a solution was possible for the case of Simple Reproduction in a 3-sector or 3-department system (producing wage-goods, or workers' subsistence, means of production and luxuries consumed by capitalists). (Actually, Bortkievicz acknowledged the primacy in a crucial respect of the neglected Russian writer, Dmitriev, who had published a study of Ricardo's theory of value three years before, in 1904 in Moscow). An incidental curiosity of this Bortkievicz solution was that it was independent of the conditions of production of this third sector producing for capitalist consumption: it depended exclusively on the conditions of production of the other two sectors – a result which, he claimed, demonstrated that profit was the fruit of exploitation (or had the nature of a 'deduction' as he preferred to call it) and had nothing to do with the productivity of capital. It is only during the last ten years that a solution has been demonstrated for the *n*-product case – i.e. shown to be possible for an indefinitely large number of commodities – by Francis Seton of Oxford in the *Review of Economic Studies* in 1956-7 – a demonstration that (in his own words) 'the logical superstructure' of Marx's theory is 'sound enough'. This some might consider the more convincing because Dr Seton was at pains to dissent from the theory of surplus-value. Such a demonstration (independently and indeed earlier arrived at) is also implicit in the equations that form the crux of the derivation of prices from conditions of production in Part One of Piero Sraffa's *Production of Commodities by Means of Commodities* (published seven years ago [1960]).

There are two incidental questions of a theoretical but more general nature on which I should have liked to dwell, if only because these quite widely concern economics students when they come into contact with Marx's writings. Both refer to the relation between Marx's theory and what some call 'modern economics' (as taught in the schools) and others call 'bourgeois economics'. For obvious reasons I cannot do justice to either of these questions here. Yet, lest I be chided for avoiding them altogether, I will attempt a very brief, rather dogmatic and doubtless inadequate answer as concisely as I possibly can.

Firstly, a question may be asked about the relation between the two: are they mutually exclusive in their entirety? Does acceptance of the one mean total rejection and negation of the other? Does a Marxist deny that there is anything at all to be learned from what economists have written since, say, 1870 – which would be equivalent to saying that *no* dialogue between the schools is possible? The only short answer I can give to this is to say that there is no simple 'Yes' or 'No' answer, and that either a wholly 'Yes' or a wholly 'No' answer unqualified would be both *simpliste* and wrong. It would be as absurd to deny that any contributions even of a formal character (e.g. in econometrics and input-output analysis) have been made by economists of the present century as to represent them all (as has sometimes been done) as 'a homogenous reactionary mass'. If the concept of 'demand elasticity' had been invented in his day, Marx would doubtless have made some, if perhaps subordinate, use of it in his treatment of market-price (as it is being utilized in socialist countries today); and he might well have made some use of some modern analyses of monopoly, semi-monopoly and so-called 'oligopoly' situations in his references to monopoly-price. Even the notion of marginal increments or decrements cannot be regarded as the special monopoly of the Subjective Theory of Value: borrowed as it is from the differential calculus it can properly have a place in the handling of any problem concerned with maxima or minima (so-called 'extremal problems'). Again, I don't think there can be much doubt that at least some recent discussion of growth-models, especially controversies over their alleged stability or instability, is of considerable interest to Marxists – even if the creators of such models are apt to be excessively fond of explanation in terms of 'propensities', to concentrate too exclusively on a purely income-expenditure or demand-sided approach and to play down or obscure the conditions and structure of production. (Certain by-products of discussion of such growth-models – in particular modern critique of the marginal productivity theory of distribution and of the notion of measurability of capital as a factor of production should *certainly* be of interest). I am reminded of some words of Rosa Luxemburg to the effect that 'the scrupulous endeavour to keep "within the bounds of Marxism" may at times have been just as disastrous to the integrity of the thought process as has been the other extreme – complete repudiation of the Marxist outlook and the determination to manifest 'independence of thought' at all hazards.

But an economic theory is *not* just a collection of analytical techniques or 'box of tools' (in Schumpeter's handy phrase it is essentially a '*vision*' of what economic society is like and how it functions); and to be blind to the fact that much if not most of modern economic theory has been so shaped as to exclude and render meaningless such questions as Marx was mainly concerned with (so that they just can't be talked about) – in particular, surplus-value and exploitation, and the essence of social relations *behind* market-appearances – this would be no less absurd and damaging; and certainly obscurantist and wrong-headed. Towards a whole system of capitalist apologetics of this kind it would be surprising, indeed, if Marxism did not turn a sharply critical edge.

The second question, following closely on the heels of the first, is concerned with the possibility of 'reconciliation'. Is there not some wider synthesis in which the 'truths' of both can be combined? It is sometimes said, especially by mathematically-minded economists today, that in any all-embracing system of general equilibrium (of the so-called Walrasian type) *both* conditions of production *and* conditions of demand must inevitably be specified, explicitly or by implication. Accordingly, looked at from *one* end it can be treated as a labour theory of value, looked at from the *other* end it can be interpreted as a theory of marginal utility (relative prices, that is, must bear a definite relation to both). Again, the only short answer I can give is one that may seem to some of you to beg a lot of questions. In a *purely formal* sense it is probably true to say that this kind of apparent 'reconciliation' or synthesis is quite possible. In a system of equations all the unknowns are determined equally by all the relationships (or conditions) defined by the equations; and what one singles out as 'independent' and what as 'dependent' variables is, from a formal standpoint, arbitrary. Marx did not deny that consumers' demand came into the picture; nor could theorists of the utility or subjective school omit all reference to circumstances of production (although they *did* to social or *class* relations of production). But an economic theory is *not* and *cannot* be a purely formal structure, concerned exclusively with quantitative relations in their pure form; and as soon as one starts infusing it with economic content, questions of *causation* inevitable come in (even if it be causation of a complex rather than a simple uni-directional kind). It becomes something *more* than just a system of equations of general equilibrium: it becomes a matter of how one pictures the general shape of things and their 'modus operandi'; of what is of primary consequence and what secondary, of what it is that sets the limits of the *possible* – to put it crudely, of 'which in practice changes what' in an operational sense. It is in *this* kind of question, about the essential nature of economic society and about causal sequences, that the essential difference between Marxian Political Economy and the other Schools of Political Economy consists.

To return to the structure and content of Marx's *Capital* and the circumstances in which it was written – from which some may think I have digressed too far. One remark about Marx's method cannot be omitted: namely, that while his purpose and interest in this work was primarily theoretical, he resembled Adam Smith (and indeed went beyond him) in the extent to which he mingled abstract reasoning with historical data of a very concrete and detailed character. This was manifestly part of the central design of the work and was fully consonant with his general attitude towards the relations of theory to actuality: combination of the two served to reveal the general in the particular and to establish the categories of his thought as representations of the essence of real human activity, not abstractions empty of life. Thus we have in Volume I those richly factual excursions into reports of 19th century factory inspectors and government blue books about working conditions and wage-payment and the effects of machinery; also the famous historical data on methods of 'primitive accumulation' in Part VIII. In Volume III there are the historical excursions into different forms of rent, with the distinctive types of social relations of which these are the expression; into Merchant Capital, rich in detailed hints and suggestions (it is here that we find the brief reference to the 'two roads' of transition to bourgeois methods of production, which to my mind unlocks many doors; also the pregnant phrase about 'the way in which surplus value is pumped out of the direct producers' as affording always the explanation of 'the relation between rulers and ruled'). To this one should add the pages of data about interest and credit with its references to Thomas Tooke's *History of Prices* and *An Inquiry into the Currency Principle*, to official enquiries into the financial crisis of 1847-8 and to evidence before the Select Committee on Bank Acts.

One cannot pass over entirely without mention three topics which, in addition to his theory of value and surplus value, have been the subject of comment and controversy. First, there are his references to the impoverishment of the working class in Chapter XXV of Volume I: the chapter entitled 'The General Law of Capitalist Accumulation'. This is the origin of the so-called 'tendency to absolute impoverishment of the working class' around which there has been so much questioning and debate. Secondly, there are the chapters in Volume III on the Falling Rate of Profit and on counteracting tendencies to it. Thirdly, there is the famous schema of reproduction in the third part of Volume II: a set of arithmetical tables depicting in two-sectional or two-departmental form the equilibrium relations needing to be observed under conditions of 'simple' and 'expanded reproduction' respectively – and in doing so indicating the improbability of such conditions being maintained except 'by accident' in a system characterized by 'anarchy of production'. These reproduction schema were to become the centre of attention in the debate between rival interpretations of the causation of crises, most notably in Rosa Luxemburg's polemical theory (with its emphasis on market-demand and so-called 'realisation' of surplus value) and the contrasted (indeed opposed) theory of Tugan-Baranovsky which laid stress on the possibility of an uninhibited process of expanded reproduction, which Rosa Luxemburg had denied.

Since the publication of the *Grundrisse der Kritik der Politischen Oekonomie*, a manuscript of 1857-8, which contained a preliminary version of the schema, we know that this notion of setting out the structural inter-relationships of production in a tabular form was present in Marx's mind at a relatively early date, before the actual publication of his *Kritik der Politischen Oekonomie* in 1859. It is interesting to note, moreover, that the schema in the *Grundrisse* of 1857-8, in its breakdown into sectors, distinguishes production of raw materials from production of machinery among means of production, and among means of consumption separates output of necessaries for workers from luxuries or surplus products for capitalists.

What is significant, of course, is not the number of sectors he chose, but the crucial role he assigned to the structural interrelations of the production process. In present-day language, what we manifestly have in the Reproduction Schema is a provisional and embryonic form of an input-output matrix or table, of which the totals of columns and rows bear a necessary relation to one another.

It was in November 1866 (as Franz Mehring tells us) that 'the first bundle of manuscript' of Volume I of *Das Kapital* was sent off to Hamburg, to 'a publisher of democratic literature' called Otto Meissner. This was followed five months later by the remainder of the manuscript which was taken to Hamburg by Marx in person. The final proof-sheets were corrected on 16th August 1867 – 'at two o'clock in the morning' as he told Engels – and returned to the printer. The preface to the first German edition is dated 25th July of that year, and the book was published early in September. (By mid-September copies of it had reached Marx and he was dispatching inscribed copies to his friends).

The first volume was the product of work over nearly two decades – work interrupted and rendered intermittent both by illness and by political preoccupations, including the foundation of the First International. His acquaintance with the English economists of the classical school dates back to his days in Paris (his first exile) in the middle 1840s. But intensive study and writing about political economy and capitalism date from his domicile in London from 1850. Here it was that he made the Reading Room of the British Museum his workshop; his writing being mainly done at home – at first in the cramped Soho lodgings occupied by his family for six years and after that in modest but somewhat more capacious and pleasant surroundings in the neighbourhood of Haverstock Hill. Already in 1851 we find him writing to Engels: 'I am now so far that I have finished with all the drudgery of economics ... It is beginning to bore me. The science of political economy has made no fundamental progress since the days of Adam Smith and David Ricardo'. But this mood was not to last for long, and he was very soon back at the study of the history of political economy in the British Museum. His intention, however, of completing work on his book at an early date was frustrated. 'Especially is the time at my disposal', he explains, 'cut down by the imperative necessity of working for a living'. In December 1857 he writes: 'I am working like mad all through the nights putting my economic studies together'. This produced the *Zur Kritik* of 1859 as a kind of interim product or instalment. But again some seven years later, in a letter to Dr Kugelmann, it is: 'as for my book, I am working 12 hours a day at writing out a fair copy', a few months after which he complains: 'I cannot work productively more than a very few hours a day without feeling the effect physically ... [and] my work is often interrupted by adverse external circumstances'.

It seems to have been by the beginning of 1866 that the design of the first volume, and the intention of publishing it separately, took shape in his mind. In that year he wrote to the same Dr Kugelmann: 'my circumstances (physical and external interruptions without intermission) make it necessary for the first volume to appear separately, not both volumes together, as I had at first intended' (Letter of 13 Oct. 1866). He proceeds to explain 'how the whole work is divided':

BOOK I The Production Process of Capital
BOOK II Circulation Process of Capital
BOOK III Form of the Process as a Whole

adding that 'the first volume contains the first two books'. According to Mehring, it was between January 1866 and March 1867 that the final writing of the manuscript for Volume I was done.

As you well know, Marx did not complete the other volumes during his lifetime. These were to be published by Engels (who outlived him by 12 years), Vol. II in 1885, two years after Marx's death, and Vol. III in 1894. These parts of the manuscript were left on Marx's death as incomplete drafts and in some cases only as notes, which Engels faithfully and laboriously pieced together into the form in which we know the two volumes. As he tells us in the Preface to Vol. II, 'At best one single manuscript (No. IV) had been revised throughout and made ready for the press'. It was in this Preface, incidentally, that Engels gave a foretaste of what Volume III would contain, in these words: 'As a matter of fact, equal capitals, regardless of the quantity of actual labour employed by them, produce equal average profits in equal times. Here we have, therefore, a clash with the law of value, which was noticed by Ricardo himself, but which his school was unable to reconcile'.

Marx's work on the history of economic thought, upon which he had already started in the early 1850s, and which was intended at one time as a sequel to the *Kritik* and later as a 4th Volume of *Capital*, was not to appear even during the lifetime of Engels. The manuscript of it formed part, apparently, of the general manuscript of 1861-3, now in the possession of the Marx-Engels-Lenin Institute in Moscow, and is what we know as the *Theorien über den Mehrwert* (Theories of Surplus Value), an English translation of which has just been completed by the joint efforts of Emile Burns, Renate Simpson and Jack Cohen, of which the first part has already appeared and the rest will shortly appear.

In lieu of a peroration one can scarcely do better than to quote Rosa Luxemburg's comment on these posthumous volumes in a section which she contributed to Mehring's classic biography of Marx:

> In these circumstances we must not look to the last two volumes of *Capital* to provide us with a final and completed solution of all economic problems. In some cases these problems are merely formulated, together with an indication here and there as to the direction in which one must work to arrive at a solution. In accordance with Marx's whole attitude, his *Capital* is not a Bible containing final and unalterable truths, but rather an inexhaustible source of stimulation for further study, further scientific investigations and further struggles for truth.

She concludes the section, after referring to the 'treasures [that] still remain unmined in the 2nd and 3rd volumes' and 'a wealth of intellectual stimulation and intellectual profundity [which] they offer the enlightened workers', by saying:

> Incomplete as the two volumes are, they offer more than any final truth could: an urge to thought, to criticism and self-criticism, and this is the essence of the lessons which Marx gave the working class (Mehring, *Karl Marx*, p380).

And elsewhere (in a still earlier article) she had written:

> Marx's creation, which as a scientific achievement is a titanic whole, transcends the plain demands of the proletarian class struggle for whose purposes it was created. Both in his detailed and comprehensive analysis of capitalist economy, and in his method of historical research, with its immeasurable field of application, Marx has offered much more than was directly essential for the practical conduct of the class war ... It is not true that, as far as the practical struggle is concerned, Marx is out-of-date ... On the contrary, Marx in his scientific creation has outstripped us as a party of practical fighters.

The discussions of the 1920s about building socialism

Previous to 1917 there had been no clearly delineated picture in men's minds as to the form that a socialist economy, and more broadly a socialist society, would take. Marxism (unlike Utopian Socialism) had not even laid down any principles – apart from the fact that socialism would be established by 'the proletariat organised as the ruling class', which would forthwith 'convert the means of production into State property'; that, in some way not clearly defined, the socially-organised producers would plan production to the end of social needs; and that there would be successively a lower and higher stage of socialism or communism, in the former of which producers would be remunerated from the common pool in proportion to the quality and quantity of the work they had severally performed. As Lenin once said, 'in Marx there is no trace of attempts to create Utopias, to guess in the void at what cannot be known'; and it was only a desire to purge what he deemed to be demagogic and alien conceptions from the draft programme of the united German Social Democratic Workers' Party that caused Marx to be as explicit as he was in the famous *Critique of the Gotha Programme*.[1]

Even less was there any picture as to how the foundations of socialism were to be laid when the proletariat seized political power on the heels of a bourgeois-democratic revolution in a country that was relatively backward economically, was predominantly agricultural and had little developed industry. It is a misconception to suppose (as is all too common) that Marxism stipulated that the proletariat could seize power and start to revolutionise the social relations of production *only* in the most advanced countries where capitalism was most mature. It postulated that capitalism must have developed sufficiently to have created an industrial proletariat and brought it to a stage of class consciousness and organisation. Thereafter the possibility of social revolution depended on circumstances which so sharpened the class-antagonisms of capitalist society as to produce an explosive political situation. This could be at a relatively advanced or a not-so-advanced stage, according to the particular circumstances of this or that country, conditioning the character and rate of its economic growth, the shifts and attitudes of intermediate classes or strata (in particular the petite-bourgeoisie). Marx himself even toyed with the idea that in Russia it might be possible for capitalist development to be largely, if not entirely, bye-passed, and the transition to socialism occur on the heels of a purely bourgeois-democratic revolution which had the peasantry as its main driving-force.[2] After the appearance of Lenin's theory of Imperialism at any rate, Marxist thought was prepared for the possibility that the breakdown of capitalism might come first, not in an advanced imperialist country, but in 'the weakest link' of the system, least able to withstand the impact of an economic crisis or of war.

In the early months of the Soviet revolution the construction of socialism can hardly be said to have been on the agenda at all. Writing on *The Threatening Catastrophe and How to Avert it* in September 1917, Lenin had spoken of the institution of 'state capitalism', designed to exercise control over capitalism and over petty commodity production (i.e. peasant agriculture) alike, as the economic instrument of a 'revolutionary democratic state'. Apart from the nationalisation of the banks and of the syndicates (or sales cartels) the main immediate measure he contemplated was the compulsory union of industrial and trading firms into associations to facilitate control over them. In arguing against the Left Communists in May 1918 he wrote:

> At present, petit-bourgeois capitalism prevails in Russia, and it is *one and the same road* that leads from it to large-scale state capitalism *and* to Socialism, through *one and the same* intermediate station called 'national accounting and control of production and distribution'. Those who fail to understand this are committing an unpardonable mistake in economics [...]. State capitalism is immeasurably superior economically to the present system of economy [...]. The teachers of Socialism spoke of a whole period of transition from capitalism to socialism.

True in the first six months after October nationalisation of industry extended further than the policy-slogan of 'state capitalism' implied. But this occurred more because circumstances forced it upon the Government despite its theory and its policy-intentions than for *doctrinaire* reasons. Some of it, for example, was designed to combat non-cooperation or actual sabotage by existing owners or managerial staff; some of it was the result of direct action by workers' factory committees or enthusiastic local Soviets, presenting the central government with a *fait accompli*. A decree of Dec. 18th, 1917, had listed certain reasons for which a particular enterprise could be taken over, which included the key importance of the enterprise to the State and refusal by the owner to operate it or to observe the terms of the Decree on Workers' Control.[3] But it was not until the early summer that a whole industry as such was nationalised; and by that time the outbreak of civil war was imminent.[4]

There were, of course, those among the Bolsheviks at this period, especially those associated with the 'Left Communists', who were eager, in the name of 'permanent revolution', to press on from the stage of the bourgeois revolution to that of the socialist revolution, which they held must follow close upon the heels of the former.[5] Here there was some difference of viewpoint, at least of emphasis. Bukharin, for one, dissented from Lenin's notion that the present period was one of State Capitalism (only), declaring that State Capitalism presupposed a *capitalist*, and not a workers' State. What really forced the pace of events, however, and precipitated more extensive measures of a 'socialist' character, was the outbreak of civil war and the onset of the 'war of intervention' in the course of June and July 1918; after which the progressive slide into the system that came to be known as 'war communism' was the result of *ad hoc* improvisation under the pressure of war-needs and of the chaos occasioned by war and invasion; even if at the time it was given a *post hoc* theoretical justification. There were plenty of people who rashly hailed the extreme centralisation of the period, with its system of State-organised barter and rationed supply-allocation, as the early dawn of the new era. Even the hyper-inflation of the war years came to be justified retrospectively as a weapon for undermining the bourgeois order: *vide* Preobrazhensky's notorious reference to the printing presses as 'the machine gun of the Commissariat of

Finance attacking the bourgeois system in the rear and using the currency laws of that system to destroy it'. But as Mr E. H. Carr has said, this was simply 'an *ex post facto* justification of a course which was followed only because no means could be found of avoiding it'.[6] The authoritative verdict in retrospect came from Lenin. Looking back on it in 1921, he was to sum up the economic policy of the civil war years as follows: 'War Communism was thrust upon us by war and ruin. It was not, nor could be, a policy that corresponded to the economic tasks of the proletariat. It was a temporary measure.'[7] And again, a few months later, he referred to it as a 'mistake' and a 'jump', 'in complete contradiction to all we wrote concerning the transition from capitalism to socialism'.[8]

The New Economic Policy, introduced in 1920 as successor to 'War Communism', was officially described by Lenin as a return to the 'transitional mixed system' of State Capitalism that had characterised the first six to eight months of the October Revolution. But the first few years of the decade of the '20s were fully preoccupied with the tasks of reconstruction – with wooing peasant agriculture, now free to trade its surplus (after payment of Agricultural Tax), to increase production and supply the towns; and with overcoming the bottlenecks of transport and of fuel that were threatening to paralyse industrial production. It was not for some years that either the situation was ripe or men's minds had the chance or the inclination for consideration of policy in general terms: for posing the question of 'where next?' from this 'transitional mixed system' of the NEP and viewing the perspective of future development. For socialist thought and socialist polemics this was something quite new. Not only the pattern of the future socialist society and even its guiding principles had previously been unexplored, but even the road by which such a society could be reached from the historical stage that Russia was in at this date was something that had not previously been the subject of serious enquiry. In this sense it is true that no one had contemplated the problem of how to build socialism in a country where the industrial revolution, although it had begun, remained uncompleted, where factory industry employed no more than between two and three million, four-fifths of the population derived their livelihood from agriculture, and no more than 15 per cent of the population was urban. Other brands of Socialists, particularly the Mensheviks, were stoutly denying the possibility of any transition to Socialism until a whole historical period of bourgeois hegemony had served to complete the industrialisation of the country on a capitalist basis; and it was for this reason that they had accused Lenin and the Bolsheviks of 'Blanquism' in having prematurely seized power in the name of the Soviets.

From the early days of the revolution and before, Lenin had, of course, been perfectly clear that large-scale industry, and its extension beyond its existing small extent, was the essential economic basis for the construction of a socialist society in a backward, partially industrialised country. For him this was almost axiomatic and was the reason for his harping on the postulate, in 1918 and again in 1921, that 'Socialism is inconceivable without large-scale capitalist technique based on the last word of modern science' and for emphasising against impatient 'dreamers' what had traditionally been said about 'prolonged birth pangs' of the new social order, extending over 'a whole period of transition from Capitalism to Socialism'. But hitherto it had been commonly assumed among the Bolsheviks that a pre-requisite of such an essential next step was a spread of the revolution to Central and Western Europe: a view which Lenin had apparently shared, or at least had hitherto seen no occasion to call in question. It was only after Stalin in 1924 propounded 'the possibility of building socialism in one country' that revolution in the west as a necessary premise for the completion of industrialisation in Russia was seriously or extensively questioned.

Industrialisation of the country went on record as an agreed principle – as the essential next step before a transition to socialism could be made – at the 14th Party Congress of December 1925; this affirmation of the 'possibility of socialism in one country' following on a keen debate with Trotsky and the opposition within the Party both at this Congress and at the preliminary conference of the Party in April of the year.[9] But it was one thing to affirm the possibility of industrialisation, and quite another to demonstrate how this could be done. Industrialisation, in the first place, requires extensive capital investment; and this raises the question of the *sources* of the requisite investible funds. Obviously, in the circumstances of Soviet Russia in the 1920s, the answer could not lie in the direction of import of foreign capital (even in the form of long-term commercial credits on any substantial scale). Expressed in real terms (i.e. in terms of productive resources and productive possibilities) the question of *sources* of capital accumulation raised a series of questions, such as how the marketed surplus of agricultural products, supplied by the villages to the towns, could be increased in a sufficient measure to supply the needs of a growing industry and a growing population of industrial workers. Could such an increase be assured at all on the basis of a primitive and small-scale peasant agriculture? Did not a sufficient increase, to make a growth of industry and of industrial employment possible, presuppose a prior revolution in the conditions of agriculture – in its institutional basis and also probably in its technical conditions as well? The question was also raised of the effect of industrialisation on the foreign trade balance. If machinery and constructional equipment had to be imported because they could not immediately be produced at home, then (apart from pruning luxury imports or foreign borrowing) this would require a corresponding expansion of exports: whence was this increased exportable surplus to come? This brought one back again to agriculture and its potential surplus; also to an acute political issue, whether the restricted consumption which an enlarged exportable surplus must entail should fall primarily on the urban working class, which had formed the spearhead of the revolution, or on its essential ally the peasantry. The former was an unthinkable demand to ask the workers voluntarily to accept after the hunger and suffering they had endured in the civil war years – the very class in whose interests and to alleviate whose lot the revolution had been made. The latter was to invite peasant passive resistance, in the form of a withholding of their grain, as had been their answer to war-time requisitioning; if not to invite a peasant *La Vendée*, bringing a counter-revolutionary holocaust in its train. One did not have to be abnormally faint-hearted to feel that an impasse had been reached, and that nothing short of a resurgence of the German revolutionary wave could save the Russian revolution from stagnation or retrogression.

Discussion centred around such issues was in part a debate between economic experts confronted with a series of practical and theoretical questions that economic analysis had never previously faced, at least not in their present form. This debate has been described by a recent writer in America as 'a singularly exciting chapter in the history of economic doctrines; a chapter which is particularly worth exploring at a time when long-range growth has come again, after the lapse of nearly a century, to be one of the key concerns of economics, and when the presence of political elements in large economic decisions no longer causes apprehension.' The same writer goes on to say:

> To be sure, the economist of today who follows these discussions cannot help being frequently dismayed by the unsystematic nature of the argument [...]. Moreover, the leading debaters rarely take the trouble to buttress their diagnosis by statistical data. Yet a Western student who, on account of technical inadequacies, disregards the ability of the Soviet theorists of the Twenties to ask pertinent questions and to put forward suggestive solutions, refuses to see an imposing forest behind not-too-well-kept trees [...]. The debate of the Twenties lays a serious claim to our attention, also, on the grounds of its intrinsic merits alone. But it is idle to deny that this claim is immeasurably strengthened by the momentous nature of the actions which followed the words. The Soviet economic advance since 1928 has been one of the dominant facts of our time [...]. According to the virtually unanimous view of Western students, the expansion of the Soviet industrial capacity has proceeded at a rate, which is, by any meaningful standard of comparison, unprecedented.[10]

But the discussion was not and could not be confined to economists. Inevitably in the circumstances of the time, since it touched vital issues of the very survival of the revolution and the very possibility of socialism, it became a burning debate within the government and the ruling Party. Moreover the issues in debate were destined to become the focal point of fierce and bitter clashes between rival groups and divergent trends within the Party: in particular between the trends associated respectively with the names of Trotsky and of Stalin. Perhaps the purely economic differences could have been reconciled, ultimately at least, and need not have widened to the point where faction-fights, splits and expulsions from the Party became the order of the day. It is vain and pointless to speculate as to whether the outcome would have been different if the leading personalities had been other than what they were – if, for example, Lenin, with his genius for mediation as well as for sharp polemic, had chanced to live for another ten years; or again, if the advice of Lenin's Testament about the

General-Secretaryship of the Party had been taken. The fact is that the differences reached a point where they became irreconcilable; and as one looks back on these years from a greater distance it becomes plain that what parted the disputants into opposing camps and precluded compromise between them was a difference in socio-political conception of the whole character and the setting of the transition to socialism in a country situated as was Russia at the time. The dispute was not simply one about the economic means best adapted to progress rapidly along an agreed road. The very road of development was in dispute, and even the direction in which it lay. At times it seemed that there might also be lack of agreement as to the nature of the goal at which the revolution was aiming (in the sense of the definition, and the constituent elements, of a socialist society, and accordingly how one could recognise that one had reached it). But that this was really so is less clear. Allowing for the changes made in the world-context of discussion by the lapse of three decades and the impact of a world war, one could perhaps detect certain parallels between the divergence of conceptions then and the divergence between Soviet and Chinese conceptions today. 'Permanent Revolution' and 'Socialism in One Country', the two slogan-phrases round which discussion focussed, much as they have both suffered from uninformed or twisted interpretation, were more than empty phrases, used as shuttlecock of heated debate: they stood as labels for divergent conceptions, or at least of conceptions having a different focus and emphasis, even if these conceptions were never fully worked out (at the time at least) and explicitly defined. But there can be no doubt that in the one much greater reliance was placed on the spread of proletarian revolution to the West (and hence on the need to force the pace of revolution abroad), and correspondingly a greater dread of the reactionary potentialities of peasant economy and a more hostile attitude towards it. Thus the proletarian-peasant alliance – the *smytchka* on which Lenin was always insisting – was viewed by those who leaned towards the doctrine of 'permanent revolution' as a temporary expedient, enduring only for a period, and not as a continuing foundation-stone in the construction of socialism. That some day, not too far off, the proletarian march towards socialism must inevitably clash with, even decisively 'settle with', the peasantry, was doubtless at the back of the minds of many of the 'Left opposition' of those years, even if it was seldom formulated in so many words.[11] If so, how could this prospect be faced without socialist allies to fall back upon in the more advanced countries of the West – countries having a proletariat that was numerically stronger as well as more mature culturally and politically? Yet it was this very prospect that the doctrine of 'socialism in one country' by implication rejected.

The economic issues of the middle and late 1920s and the policy-differences towards them first came to light in the so-called 'scissors crisis' of 1923. The economic difficulties experienced in the summer and autumn of that year were so-called because of a diverging trend of the prices of agricultural products and the prices of industrial products: when depicted on a graph the curves representing these trends evoked the kind of image which the term 'scissors' implied. For some months the gap between the two continued to widen, agricultural prices falling and industrial prices as steadily rising. During the summer of 1923 sales of industrial goods had been declining, especially in village markets and in rural townships; and by October (the month of the widest opening of the 'scissors') the ratio of industrial to agricultural prices stood at more than 3:1 as compared with the ratio that had prevailed in pre-war days (treated as 1:1). This represented a drastic shift in the terms of trade between industry and agriculture to the disadvantage of the latter. Not unnaturally this resulted in a reluctance of peasants to market their grain, coupled with mutterings of peasant discontent, and on the other hand in complaints from industrial and trading organisations of 'glutted markets' and 'over-production' and mounting stocks of unsaleable goods. It came to be spoken of (e.g. by Rykov at the 13th Party Conference in 1924) as 'the first crisis of the New Economic Policy' – and one which had 'driven a serious wedge between the workers and the peasants'.

In face of this situation there was official talk of the urgent need to 'close the scissors', and a special commission was set up to this end. But the question *how* this could be done depended on a prior diagnosis of the reasons for the price-phenomenon; and this diagnosis was itself affected by different interpretations of the character and future course of the existing system of the NEP. Actually the liquidation of the immediate crisis was fairly quick – a matter of a few months; and it was largely achieved by administrative measures directed towards the adjustment of prices. Grain was purchased for export by State buying organs; and agricultural prices rose abruptly between the harvest and the end of the year (and by the spring of 1924 they were almost double what they had been six months before). In October the Commissariat for Internal Trade commenced a series of price-reduction orders to industrial and trading organisations (starting with the Textile Syndicate); and this, combined with the effect of a credit-squeeze from the side of the State Bank (which encouraged an unloading of stocks), was successful in effecting substantial price-reductions on the part of industry. Disagreement remained, however, and discussion was to continue as to whether from a long-term point of view the closing of the scissors in this way was a correct solution. By the spring of 1924 the immediate crisis of the scissors could be said to be a thing of the past; industrial production was expanding, and a monetary reform designed to halt inflation was in train.[12]

Attention to the disparate movement of agricultural and industrial prices had first been drawn, as a matter of fact, by Trotsky in a report on industry to the 12th Party Congress in April 1923, at a time when the opening of the 'scissors', although pronounced, had not yet reached anything like its full extent.[13] At the time, however, attention was focussed primarily on general currency inflation, and the only policy-conclusions immediately drawn, in view of the widening gap between industrial and agricultural prices, were the promotion of grain exports and the need to increase industrial efficiency and to reduce costs by measures of industrial concentration (i.e. concentrating production on the larger and more efficient plants). But already in the discussion at this Congress, and preceding it, there began to be discernible a grouping of opinion into two broad camps. The first of these (represented at the time by the official reports of Kamenev and Zinoviev at the Congress) laid prior emphasis on the development of agriculture – on giving every possible latitude and encouragement to the peasantry to expand their cultivated area and to market their produce. This, it was assumed, was the economic cornerstone of the NEP and must be the continuing priority of the coming years. Only on this basis of expanded commodity interchange between agriculture and industry, town and country, could industrial reconstruction proceed and eventually the growth of industry be resumed. (Kamenev in his report on peasant taxation affirmed the 'mutual relations between the proletariat and the peasantry' to be 'the basic problem of the dictatorship of the proletariat in the present period'.[14]) The second group of opinion, *per contra*, was inclined to lay prior emphasis on expansion of industry, and especially on heavy industry (which had hitherto been backward in recovery compared with light industry); and the widening of 'the scissors' was treated as a symptom of the *under*-development of industry. Coupled with this emphasis went a distrust of NEP and of the 'free market' and the acquisitive tendencies inherent in it; and consequently a desire to see this situation and policy terminated, or at least modified, as soon as possible. Trotsky in his speech at the Congress spoke of the New Economic Policy, by implication, as being non-socialist, and looked to its eventual replacement by a socialist policy through an extension of 'the planning principle' – an extension which he evidently held to be overdue. Six months later he was being much more outspoken: he now referred to 'flagrant and radical errors of economic policy', consisting in the failure to give the planning commission (Gosplan) adequate powers and in sacrificing the interests of State industry to the requirements of financial policy.[15] 'In the struggle of State industry for conquest of the market the plan is our principal weapon,' he wrote shortly after, and the 'central task of planning' should be 'to develop State industry'.[16] In the so-called *Declaration of the Forty-Six* of October 15th repeated reference was made to the existence of an 'economic and financial' (also a 'political') crisis, to be explained 'on the one hand by the absence of planned organisational leadership in industry, and on the other hand by an incorrect credit policy'.[17]

This second standpoint, which in the polemics of the next two years came to be known as that of 'the dictatorship of industry',[18] found a theoretical basis in the well-known 'theory of primitive socialist accumulation' propounded at this time by Preobrazhensky. The gist of this theory was that, since socialism was only possible on the basis of large-scale industry (as Lenin, following Marx, had always insisted), the building of socialism in a relatively underdeveloped country presupposed an initial period of intensive capital accumulation and industrialisation. This capital accumulation, if it was to be a basis for socialist economy, must obviously be in the hands of the State, and not of private individuals (as had been the case in the genesis of capitalism): it must represent, in terms of production, the expansion of State industry itself. In financial terms this accumulation could only take the form either of taxation or of the profits of State industry. But as regards the actual *source* of this accumulation, there was an analogy with the formative days of capitalism: this source could only be the sector of petty commodity production, in other words the small producer, and this meant essentially the peasantry. (Hence the term 'primitive accumulation' to stress the analogy with the methods which Marx had described in *Das Kapital.*) Apart from taxation of the peasantry (already represented by the Agricultural Tax), the method of transferring resources into the domain of State industry must be that of turning the terms of trade, or of commodity-interchange, between industry and agriculture in favour of the former. And this was precisely what the opening of 'the scissors' had done.

This bold and ruthless conception of the road of development towards socialism – regarded as the *conditio sine qua non* of such development – was first expounded by Preobrazhensky in a paper read to the Communist Academy in 1924, and two years later in a booklet entitled *Novaia Ekonomika.* After stating that in the first place the surplus product of State industry was capable of being enlarged by raising industrial productivity and by raising wages in smaller proportion than the rise in labour productivity, he went on to emphasise that the immediate possibilities of this were strictly limited. They were limited, firstly by the low level of existing technique,[19] and secondly by the political necessity, under conditions of the dictatorship of the proletariat, to raise the standard of living of the working class (and hence real wages) as rapidly as possible. It followed (he argued) that the prime source of accumulation must, therefore, consist of

> the accumulation in the hands of the State of material means obtained mainly from sources lying outside the State economic system. [...] In a backward agrarian country this accumulation is bound to play a very great role. Primitive accumulation predominates conspicuously during this period; and we must therefore designate this whole stage [of development] as the period of primitive or preparatory socialist accumulation.[20]

These 'outside spheres' he called 'colonies'; and the characteristic relationship of this whole transitional period, while industrialisation was being intensively undertaken, must be one of 'exploitation' between the State industrial sector and these 'colonies' of petty individual production – giving to the petty producers less in value than the values they supplied to the State sector (e.g. as foodstuffs and raw materials); thereby augmenting the 'surplus value' available to State industry to provide the sinews of investment and growth.[21]

Taxation of such 'colonies' could play a limited role. But the main method he conceived as being industrial price-policy, whereby State industry made deliberate use of its monopoly position. 'The concentration of the whole of large-scale industry of the country into a single trust, that is into the hands of the Workers' State, increases to an extraordinary extent the possibility of conducting such a price policy on the basis of monopoly, a price policy signifying an alternative form of taxation of individual production.' The political significance of such a theory in the circumstances of 1923 and 1924 is quite plain.

Some Western economic writers in recent years have sought to rehabilitate Preobrazhensky as an original and discerning anticipator of the essential problems of economic growth in underdeveloped countries.[22] Some have asserted that the subsequent history of Soviet industrialisation has fully justified his central ideas, and that his only fault was lack of political tact in speaking so openly and so soon.[23]

Undoubtedly his conception was both original and arresting, and it has the merit of both clarity and boldness. In so far as his theory can be taken as stating merely that the burden of supplying the resources for industrial growth must in some sense fall upon peasant agriculture in inverse ratio to the existing level of industrial development, its truth can scarcely be disputed. There is an important sense in which, for a time at least (and in the absence of foreign borrowing), industry must inevitably build itself at the expense of agriculture; and such an 'objective necessity' can be said to govern development whether it be on a capitalist basis or under the *aegis* of Socialism. But in the first place there is room for discussion as regards the emphasis of Preobrazhensky's theory – as to the length of this period and also as to the possibilities of mobilising resources in other ways (e.g. by rationalised organisation, by concentration on priority objectives or by tapping latent reserves previously unutilised). In the second place it is clear that

Preobrazhensky's theory was saying considerably *more* than that a substantial part of the contribution to accumulation must come from the peasantry: indeed, it went substantially beyond any abstract analysis of the problem to become a specific policy-prescription. Not only did it dramatise the situation, and emphasise historical analogies by its very terminology (e.g. 'primitive accumulation', 'colonies', 'exploitation') – this, indeed, could be said to be part of its attraction; but it was framed in such a way as to point to the conclusion that 'monopolist price-policy' by State industry must be the centrepiece of economic policy in the period of industrialisation and transition to socialism. Here was a whole series of questions of practical emphasis that were much more debatable.

As soon as we ask why he made this emphasis as sharply as he did, and why it came to be employed as, in effect, an attack on the policy of restricting credit to industry and closing the scissors, hidden links with the political conception of 'permanent revolution' are discernible. Preobrazhensky and his fellow 'oppositionists' felt that they were 'working against the clock'; that the existing situation where the proletariat, leaning upon the peasantry, had seized power in an un-industrialised country, and was holding the fort against a hostile world, was inherently unstable. Unless revolution spread to the West, chronic economic crisis and counter-revolution could only be averted by resort to desperate expedients – forced industrialisation at a high rate and energetic measures to restrict individual petty production and force it to serve socialist aims. The crucial issue was the time-scale on which advance was to be plotted; and the ebbing of the revolutionary wave in Germany in 1923 served to fan a mood of defeatism among the adherents of the 'permanent revolution' *tendenz*. This atmosphere of urgency and haste was to return, of course, in the following decade after the rise of Fascism in Germany and the reappearance of the danger of war; and with this more tense atmosphere came the strategy of forced industrialisation and the 'big push'. But this was after the lapse of more than a quinquennium had brought some renewed strength to industry, the restoration at least of agricultural production (if not of its marketed surplus) to the pre-war level, the construction of an apparatus of planning and the possession of a richer experience of industrial administration. This preoccupation with the time-factor becomes plain to view in Preobrazhensky's warning to an audience at the Communist Academy that 'we shall not be given much time in which to build socialism. [...] It will be a matter of life and death that we should rush through this transition as quickly as possible.' 'We must anticipate,' he went on, 'a united campaign of the *kulaks* and world capital, launching an economic and also a military-political offensive [...]. We are constructing socialism in the situation of a lull between battles.'[24] It could be said, of course, that what was to happen sixteen years later justified this note of alarm. Sixteen years, however, represented a wider horizon than most of Preobrazhensky's colleagues in the 'Left opposition' (as it was to become) probably envisaged at the time; and much in his and in their detailed prescriptions rested on the assumption that the danger came as much from within the economy as from without. It has to be remembered that when the context of the argument is policy-prescription, the length of one's horizon is crucial: to each horizon there may well be a quite different answer, and what is right at one date, or with one degree of foresight, may be quite wrong at another. Here most of all is it true that there are no universal truths.

The answer that was made at the time to this whole line of policy, as epitomised most clearly in the theory of primitive socialist accumulation, was that nothing was more certain to disrupt the *smytchka*, or union, between industrial working class and peasantry, which had been the linchpin of Lenin's policy, and to restore which had been the *raison d'être* of the NEP. Indeed, the conception of a calculated exploitation of the peasantry by the Workers' State stood manifestly in contradiction to the very idea of such an alliance, reducing the latter to a short-term tactical manoeuvre, to be discarded as soon as the first phase of the revolution was over. Had not the scissors crisis shown the incompatibility of a monopoly price-policy by industry even with the immediate needs of reconstruction? Was there a surer way of inviting chronic economic crisis and an *impasse* in the mutual exchange-relationship between agriculture and industry? From a long-term standpoint it would be no less disastrous: it would place a permanent drag upon the growth of agriculture and of agricultural productivity by depriving the peasantry of incentive to expand production and sales. Thus (it was claimed) anything in the nature of an *ultra* interpretation of the policy of 'industry first' would have an opposite result to what was intended, since the advance of socialist industry needed to lean (on one flank at least) on the advance of agriculture; and to ignore or to retard the latter represented a one-sided, undialectical approach to the problem. It was further argued that there were larger sources of accumulation latent in rationalisation and improved organisation in industry than the advocates of monopoly price-policy for industry were willing to allow. Moreover, there were still possibilities of drawing upon the pool of unemployed labour ('turning labour into capital' to use a recent phrase, coined in relation to Chinese policy in the 1950s). But whether the scope for this without *prior* replacement and enlargement of industrial equipment was very great, even in 1924, may be doubted.

A leading spokesman for this line of criticism was Bukharin; and it was to become the official answer to the 'opposition' after the *Declaration of the Forty-Six* and the 13th Party Congress. While admitting that 'socialised industry receives a surplus value for its accumulation funds from the small producer' and that there is an element of 'transfer of values' from the latter to the former, Bukharin emphatically denied the validity of the analogy with early capitalist accumulation which Preobrazhensky had sought to draw. This denial was chiefly on the grounds that the conscious aim of Soviet policy was progressively to lessen the antagonism between proletariat and peasantry by *reducing* rather than increasing such a 'transfer of values' – reducing it in the degree to which socialist industry developed and was able to rely on 'internal accumulation' (out of its own ploughed-back profits, as the fruit of higher productivity). *Per contra*, Preobrazhensky's conception of peasant production as 'colonies' of the industrial metropolis implied a deepening and perpetuation of this antagonistic relationship. Instead of 'Monopolist Parasitism' (as Bukharin termed it), 'we shall attain our aim in a very different manner by inducing the peasantry to enter into cooperatives allied with us and economically dependent on the State and its institutions. By this we shall arrive at Socialism through the process of [market] exchange and not directly through the process of production. We shall reach Socialism through the cooperative.' It followed that, although 'it would be nonsense on our part to renounce the advantages of our monopoly position', it was vitally necessary 'not to diminish the powers of absorption of the home market but to increase these powers'. 'This' (he went on) 'is the most important point. The next is that we must utilise every advantage gained so that it may lead to an extension of the field of production and the cheapening of production, to the reduction of cost-prices and consequently to always cheaper prices in successive cycles of production.'[25]

In a statement at a later stage of the discussion,[26] Bukharin makes clear that his disagreement is less with the diagnosis, or the analysis of the problem, by Preobrazhensky than with its policy-application, namely in the following passage.

> Our State industry cannot obtain the means for its expansion solely from the labour of the working class within this State industry itself, and it must necessarily draw on the non-industrial reservoir for the means to support and expand industry. [...] The peasantry must take its share in helping the State to build up a socialist state of industry. [...] It would be entirely wrong to say industry should develop solely upon what is produced within this industry itself. [...] The whole question is: how much can we take away from the peasantry, to what extent and by what methods can we accomplish the pumping-over process, what are the *limits* of the pumping over? [...] The comrades of the opposition are in favour of an immoderate amount of pumping-over, and are desirous of putting so severe a pressure upon the peasantry that in our opinion the result would be economically irrational and politically impermissible. We do not in the least hold the standpoint that we are against this pumping-over, but our calculations are more sober; we confine ourselves to measures economically and politically adapted to their purpose.

He then goes on to say that by first encouraging agriculture in order that industry may later build on its progress:

> this policy naturally involves a somewhat slower rate of advance this year, but will be compensated later by a rapid rise in the curve of our development. But if we adopt the policy of the opposition, we fly to a high summit of capital investment during the first year, only to fall the more inevitably, and probably with a very abrupt drop. We can by no means guarantee our progress by these means.[27]

In the following years the focus of discussion and disagreement shifted towards the question of whether the revival of agriculture, following the closing of the scissors, was serving to strengthen unduly the position of the *kulak*, or rich peasant, and hence to generate tendencies towards a revival of capitalist relations in the village to an extent sufficient to constitute a serious danger, against which special measures should be taken. This was the charge that the Left Opposition was to raise in 1925 at the 14th Party Congress and to continue to make in the ensuing years. (The difference of alignment now was that Trotsky, Preobrazhensky and other adherents of the 'dictatorship of industry' standpoint were now joined by Zinoviev and Kamenev and the 'Leningrad opposition' who had previously opposed the former group.) Following the scissors crisis, it had been the official policy to conciliate the peasantry by a series of measures, which included the curtailing of 'administrative measures' for dealing with the peasantry reminiscent of 'war communism', and also a relaxation of the laws regulating the leasing of land and the employment of wage-labour, as well as a reduction of the burden of the Agricultural Tax.[28] This was done under such slogans as 'Face to the Village' and 'restoration of Soviet democracy in the countryside'.[29] Attention was also given to improvements of agricultural technique, consolidation of scattered strips, improved crop rotation, etc., with extended agricultural credit for this purpose.

It was these measures, and especially the concessions as to leasing land and hiring labour, which the new opposition claimed were giving too much leash to the *kulak* and which they denounced as 'a retreat'. The *kulak*, it was argued, was in any case the main gainer from the quickened trade-turnover between village and town, since he had most grain to sell, and moreover was in a position to hold it until late in the agricultural year when he could get the best price for it; and it was he who took advantage of the concessions concerning leasing of land and hiring labour so as to enlarge his enterprise. He could afford to invest in implements and livestock and to improve his methods of cultivation, where his poorer neighbours could not. Evidence was adduced to indicate that in many areas he was on the way to resuming his pre-revolutionary economic role as grain trader and usurer to poorer peasants. Estimates of the number of *kulak* households varied, from 4 per cent of all peasant households (about one million in all), which was an official estimate in 1925, up to a figure of about double that number (sometimes even 10 per cent was mentioned).[30] This upper ten per cent, whether all were to be classed as *kulaks* or no, probably concentrated in their hands some 40 per cent of agricultural means of production and a third of the draught animals.[31]

During the next few years sensitiveness to this *kulak* danger was to remain the chief preoccupation of policy; and shifting appreciation of its gravity was to be largely responsible (as we shall see) for the policy-shifts of the second half of the decade. Evidently reluctance to 'rekindle the class struggle in the village' (the prevailing fear at the 14th Party Conference) very much depended on one's estimate of the *kulak*'s present strength and rate of growth. Among the supporters of the official policy in 1925 there was far from unanimity on this matter. In the Centre, between Left and Right, were those who took a cautious, and largely empirical, attitude to the whole question; repudiating what they regarded as the alarmist and 'exaggerated' views of the Left and showing a willingness to tolerate the *kulak* for a little, while at the same time being quite aware that he remained an ever-present danger, but hoping to isolate him in the village and reduce his influence by winning over the 'middle peasant' to Soviet policy and by building a network of agricultural cooperatives to assist the latter and to compete with *kulak* influence as trader and money-lender.[32] Such a Centre position, however, shaded off to the Right in various degrees of 'softness' towards the *kulak*, and to a degree of tolerance that was willing to see him as a permanent feature of a fairly long transitional period and even as one of the props and levers in the construction of industry and hence of socialism.

On reflection it becomes clear that a conception of development laying primary emphasis on agriculture, to the point of implying that the growth of industry is *limited* by the growth of agriculture, must have a tendency inevitably to generate such a Right-wing interpretation in two crucial respects. This is what the 'Left Opposition' of the time evidently feared. In the first place, if the growth of industry was regarded as being more or less strictly limited by the advance of agriculture, and of the trade-turnover between the two, this could be held to imply that industry could not grow at more than quite a moderate pace and that anything faster than this was in some sense 'forced' (in more recent 'Western' terminology 'inflationary') and unnatural. Moreover, if the trade-turnover between industry and agriculture was the fulcrum of the process, then priority must be given as regards industry to the growth of consumption goods, since it was upon these that higher peasant-incomes were most likely to be spent (apart from agricultural implements and some building materials and possibly fertilisers). Heavy industry must take a back seat. Hence the picture emerged of a distinctly cautious, carefully equilibrated development, patterned on the traditional 'textiles first' sequence of development in the classical industrial revolutions of the 19th century.

In the second place, since the expansion of rural-urban trade-relations depended upon the growth of the marketed surplus of peasant agriculture, it followed that this expansion would be best served by an encouragement of those sections or strata of peasant farming which marketed the largest proportion of their crop. This, of course, pointed to the larger *kulak* farms, better-equipped with means of production, draught animals and probably with livestock and yielding a surplus product from the employment of hired labour. Hence one was apparently led on by the relentless logic of economic growth to the conception of socialist industry developing on the shoulders of a reviving and constantly reinvigorated class of labour-employing rich peasant farmers. A strange kind of new historical monster, in the shape of an urban advance to Socialism joined with a new Stolypin-policy in the countryside! Such was the nightmare logic from which Preobrazhensky had sought an escape with his doctrine and policy of 'primitive socialist accumulation' – at the expense of the peasantry and of the worker-peasant alliance. Here lay the frightening dilemma with which the failure of the revolution in western Europe confronted the would-be builders of Socialism in backward Russia.

This, indeed, was the direction in which Bukharin's ideas of the transition were to develop, eventuating, as we shall see, in what came to be defined before the end of the decade as a clearly-marked Right-wing tendency. Soon after the discussions of the 1923-4 period Bukharin, flushed perhaps by the success of the policy of closing the scissors, had incautiously launched his notorious *enrichissez-vous* slogan to the peasantry.[33] All too easily this could be identified – and was so identified by his critics – with an injunction to the *kulak* to grow and prosper, if not to tread again the road of Gorki's Artamanovs. (Had not Bukharin himself said, *inter alia*, 'we are helping him [the *kulak*], but he is helping us too'?) It was especially against this Bukharin-phrase that the Leningraders reacted so strongly; and the cry was raised of a 'Thermidorian danger'. So strong was the revulsion against the vista opened up by this initially innocent-seeming phrase as to cause Bukharin to withdraw it. Nonetheless, he had himself kindled a fear that was not readily appeased and was by no means imaginary. Moreover, it was undoubtedly the standpoint of many agricultural specialists, for example those in Kondratiev's Conjuncture Institute; and one writer in *Bolshevik* even wished to banish the word *kulak* as an obsolete category, 'a ghost of the old world'.

There were other places too in which Bukharin revealed something of the conservative and 'right-wing' implications of his attitude. In the discussions of 1923-4 he had spoken of 'moving ahead by *tiny*, tiny steps, pulling behind us our large peasant cart'[34]; and at the 14th Party Congress he spoke of 'moving at a snail's pace'; while Sokolnikov had spoken of the need to import consumer goods to throw them upon village markets (the so-called 'goods intervention'). At the 14th Party Conference in April 1925 (in reply to Larin who had raised the question of organising the poorer peasants against the *kulak* danger) Bukharin made the significant pronouncement that 'the *kolkhoz* is a powerful force, but it is not the highroad to socialism in the countryside. We look to the future inclusion of the peasant in our general system of socialist construction, whereas the opposition looks to a "second revolution"'; thus sketching a perspective of the NEP with peasant economy as its fulcrum, by continuous gradation progressively broadening out into socialism. In more strictly economic terms one of the more conservative advocates of this conception, Shanin (an official in the Commissariat of Finance) propounded a set of principles that must guide economic policy (principles that are reminiscent of what Anglo-American economists since the Second World War have trumpeted, in the belief that these ideas were original). In his economic analysis of the situation he painted a gloomy picture of an industrial sector which had few reserves, having already exhausted the possibilities of reconditioning old plants during the period of reconstruction and reached a position of full-capacity working of existing equipment. The existing 'goods famine', as it was termed, was evidence that industry was being developed too fast and in the wrong way – by forced investment in a situation where there was excess demand for consumer goods. Any further growth of industrial output would necessitate investment in new additions to fixed capital; and since heavy industry was little developed, this meant that the costs of new equipment must be economised on to a maximum extent. This was an additional argument, he thought, for giving priority of development to agriculture, since 'the organic composition of capital in agriculture is much lower' and 'a unit of capital invested in agriculture sets in motion eight times as much labour as in industry' and yields a larger surplus product. For analogous reasons, in the industrial sector light industry had to be given precedence over heavy industry: 'we must be very cautious about developing any industries that do not produce consumers' goods.' The upshot was that 'the supposition that in the immediate future our industry can develop at the same pace as agriculture is essentially wrong.' The first task was to increase agricultural exports and stimulate the production of consumers' goods, primarily with an eye to placing them on village markets.[35] The implication of the argument clearly was that, in so far as increased agricultural export permitted the import of machinery, this must be with an eye to expanding the capacity of light industry producing consumers' goods. Sokolnikov, speaking as Commissar of Finance, although at that time leaning towards the opposition in their protest against the *kulak* danger, spoke as follows in a speech of 1925:

> The more rapid development of agriculture in comparison with industry is not a handicap to the economic development of the country; on the contrary, it is a fundamental condition of its more rapid economic development. Contradictions between the levels attained by industry and agriculture must be resolved by going to the foreign market and realising the surplus of agricultural raw materials on the foreign market in order to organise the import of capital.

Previously to this, in a Budget speech, he had bluntly spoken of industry as 'fettered to the condition of peasant economy'.[36]

This question of priorities in development manifestly had to be settled before any serious beginning could be made with planning. Without decision on this crucial policy issue, the construction of a plan could be no more than an academic exercise, useful as experiment or rehearsal, but no more. Even if planning were to devote its main attention to industry, it would come at once against the issue of whether to give investment-preference to the growth of heavy industry or of light. Hence the furtherance of planning, which Trotsky had urged so vigorously in 1923, necessarily had to wait upon policy; and this meant that its further development depended upon resolving and closing the debate. The criticism heard at the time that the economy was still not a planned economy was true; but in the circumstances it is hard to see how the situation could have been otherwise. (Of the discussion around Gosplan and its role and of its early first attempts at planning, notably the first Control Figures in 1925, we shall have something more to say below.)

We have referred to the question of the relation between agriculture and industry as one of the disputed issues in the general controversy about roads to socialism. This question had a number of theoretical aspects which seriously exercised those with a *penchant* towards economic analysis. One of these was whether the alleged limit that agriculture imposed on industry took the form of a relationship between the output of industry and the market for it which peasant-demand constituted. In what sense was it true that the former could grow no faster than the latter? If the answer was in the affirmative, then something analogous to the constriction of Rosa Luxemburg's 'third market' (which in her theory applied as a constriction on the expansion of a capitalist industry) applied in conditions of NEP to socialist industry as well. Those who leaned towards the Right undoubtedly did interpret the relationship between industry and agriculture in some such way as this, even if they were seldom explicit about it. A raising of wages, of course, could also have created a market for an expanding industrial output; but this would have raised industrial costs and hence the prices of what was sold to the peasantry, which would have been contrary to what the advocates of a 'wooing-the-peasant' policy wished to see. The advocates of the contrary policy, however, especially Preobrazhensky, had an answer to any such talk about market-limits to the growth of industry. This was to the effect that expansion of industry itself would create a market *internal* to industry for its own products. In the first place, investment in re-equipment of factories and in new construction would create a market for capital goods (products of Marx's Department I). In the second place, every expansion of industrial employment would bring additional demand for consumer goods from the new recruits to the industrial army. In making this answer they were undoubtedly right; and in doing so they may be regarded as having anticipated those 'circular production-flow' models that have been so much utilised in discussions of economic growth in recent decades (from the von Neumann model onwards). So long as industry is growing by a process of internal accumulation (i.e. investment of its own profits), a circular process *within* its capital goods sector (i.e. internal to the Marxian Department I) will dominate the process. How far the market for consumption goods is expanding becomes a secondary matter (although some expansion will be necessary to the extent that part of the current investment is directed towards an enlargement of Department II). One can, indeed, go further than this and say that to talk of *market*-limits to industrial development gives a false perspective – and an unduly conservative perspective. In a socialist economy the limits to expansion in any given situation are limits on the side of supply, or of production, not of demand; and here Marxism, which approaches analysis of economic problems from the former standpoint, has a manifest advantage in throwing into relief the crucial factors and avoiding obscurantist modes of thought. It follows that in a process of industrial development heavy industry will occupy a pivotal position. Where import-possibilities are small, the ability of heavy industry to supply capital goods for industrial expansion may be a crucial limiting factor; and in laying the accent on this Preobrazhensky was perfectly correct, and indeed anticipated the later emphasis of the Five Year Plans, with their investment-priority for heavy industry. Whether there was another, and rather different, conditioning relationship between industry and agriculture is a matter to which we shall return.

The years immediately following the liquidation of the 'scissors crisis' witnessed a heartening revival of industrial production. The policy of concentrating production in fewer plants resulted in a fall of costs; and the downward pressure on selling prices encouraged industrial enterprises to take up the slack of excess capacity and to expand output by more intensive working of existing equipment. In the second half of 1924 the credit situation was also eased, following the successful accomplishment of the monetary reform; although there was continued, even gathering, complaint that light industry was the main beneficiary while heavy industry lagged behind. The harvest of 1924-5 was, however, a poor one; and in the following year there were difficulties in fulfilling the programme of grain collections despite an improved harvest, and there was talk of grain-hoarding by richer peasants. In face of an expansion of industrial output there were symptoms of so-called 'goods famine' (i.e. excess demand, or supply-shortages relatively to the existing level of demand). This formed the background, on the one hand, to those fears of growing *kulak* influence of which we have spoken, and, on the other hand, of talk (largely from circles round the Commissariat of Finance) about inflationary pressures provoked by a forced pace of industrialisation.

In 1926, however, there was a marked improvement in the agricultural situation: the harvest was a good one, and the surplus available for export was large enough to enable a peak of post-war grain-export to be attained. Both the total cultivated area and the gross output now approached the pre-war level. But in 1927 there were to be fresh difficulties in the trade relations between town and village (of which we shall speak further) and a drop in grain deliveries to the buying organs – difficulties that were repeated once again in the following year.

Meanwhile the end of 1925 (following the 14th Party Congress in December of that year) witnessed the close of what was officially designated as the period of reconstruction and the opening of the period of *new* construction and development. By the following December (1926) industrial production had been restored to the pre-war level; after which any further increase, as we have seen, had to come no longer from reserves of capacity or restored capacity but from new investment. At the same time there remained a lag (compared with pre-war output) in iron and steel. It was the experience of these years from 1925 to 1928 – an experience marked by both successes and new difficulties, by both triumphs and frustrations – that formed the background to the second phase of the discussions, and its even sharper disagreements, over the building of socialism in a single country, and eventuated in the sharp new turn of policy of 1928-9.

One result of the experience of these years was to demonstrate an important sense in which the development of industry was retarded by agriculture; although the relationship in question was of a rather different kind from that on which theoretical discussion had previously focussed attention. It is true that this relation was just another aspect of the exchange between town and country about which we have talked above (e.g. in connection with the narrowed market for industrial products during the 'scissors crisis' of 1923). But in the older discussion attention had been concentrated upon the *market* for industrial products, whereas what now came to occupy discussion was the *supply* of agricultural products available to industry and its labour force. It was not a matter primarily of industrial output and its destination, but of the sufficiency of industrial *inputs* (of raw materials and foodstuffs) to maintain a given rate of industrial expansion. The most striking circumstance to emerge from the experience of these years was the failure of the marketed surplus of agriculture to recover to its 'normal' level, despite the recovery of gross production to approximately the pre-war level and despite the closing of 'the scissors'. It was probably the realisation of this fact more than anything else that sounded the knell of the Right-wing conception of socialism growing gradually out of the NEP through peasant cooperation with industrialisation. It became clear that within the limits of individualist peasant agriculture industry could grow only very slowly – much too slowly for the time-scale on which the transition was envisaged. The events of 1927 and 1928 were to show that the threat of actual starvation of the town population had not been banished: that if anything it grew more serious with every enlargement of the industrial population. To end that threat was the *conditio sine qua non* of any serious policy of industrialisation.

The position at this time was that, although total grain production fell very little short of the level of the pre-war years, the surplus of grain placed on the market outside the village scarcely reached a half of the pre-war amount. The position of other crops than grain was somewhat better; but no more than 17 per cent of the total agricultural harvest was marketed, and the total of agricultural supplies (including flax and cotton etc.) placed on the market did not exceed 70 per cent of the pre-war amount, even though the total cultivated area stood at 95 per cent of pre war.[37]

The reason, of course, lay in the greater equalisation of holdings, which was the legacy of the revolution so far as the village was concerned. As a result, the peasantry were consuming a larger proportion of their produce and selling less of it to the towns. Before the revolution it was the landowners' estates and the richer *kulak* farms that supplied more than two-thirds of all the marketed grain; the former marketing something like a half of all they produced, whereas poor and middle peasants, although they accounted for a half of all the grain produced, marketed less than a sixth of it. By contrast, in the middle and later '20s, 85 per cent of all grain produced came from poor and middle peasant farms (*bedniak* and *seredniak*), and of this they marketed no more than 11 or 12 per cent, themselves consuming the remainder. *Kulak* farms amounted to no more than a quarter to one-third of their previous number, and those that existed were of smaller average size. In face of this situation the policy of reducing industrial prices during the past two years had had relatively little effect in stimulating peasant sales. It was to this fact that Stalin was to draw attention in the discussions of the ensuing year; and the policy-implication of such an emphasis was very obvious. Such State and collective farms as existed at that date marketed as large a proportion of their crop as had landlords' estates in pre-revolutionary days; but they only accounted for less than 2 per cent of total grain production. The implication clearly was that, to restore the marketed surplus even to its pre-war level, the sector of State and collective farming must be enlarged so as to have a comparable position, at least, in agriculture to that of large estate-farming before the Revolution.

The renewed difficulties in the grain market in 1927 and 1928 placed this question in the centre of political and economic discussion. We have seen that the grain situation in 1926 had been fairly good – sufficiently good for some 150 million poods to be exported out of total grain collections from the village of some 660 million.[38] Although the harvest in 1927 was again a relatively good one (the third in succession), grain collections in the late autumn began to fall substantially below the anticipated level, and by the closing months of the year had dropped to less than half of the same period of the previous year.[39] Despite some improvement in January and February, even worse was to follow in the spring of the new year, and in July, on the eve of the new harvest, a grain import of some 12 million poods became necessary (which amounted to two-thirds of all that had been exported since the previous October). At the same time the industrial 'goods famine' once more emerged. The relatively high prices paid for purchases from the village had combined with increased urban employment to raise the demand for industrial consumer goods faster than their output had risen (it was estimated that over the half-year total purchasing power had grown by nearly 12 per cent and the supply of industrial consumer goods by only 3 to 4 per cent).[40] The implication seemed to be that both the volume of new construction work and the urban standard of life were increasing faster than the economic situation would permit; and the advocates of a cautious policy, such as Shanin, seemed at first sight to be justified.

The measures immediately taken to deal with the situation were of a fairly traditional kind. There was again a restriction of credit and a curtailment of the quantity of currency in circulation. Stocks of industrial goods were diverted to village markets, and a new Industrialisation Loan was issued, in the hope that it would absorb surplus purchasing-power, especially in the village. After the new harvest of 1928 grain-prices were raised; but market conditions continued to deteriorate, and grain collections in 1928-9 were lower than the previous year and amounted to no more than two-thirds of 1926-7.

This situation was the background to the developing campaign for the collectivisation of agriculture that gathered momentum in the course of 1928 and 1929, slowly at first and then with an accelerated 'leap' in the course of 1929. These years also saw the launching of the First Five Year Plan. Parallel with this new current of events went an inevitable sharpening of conflict and eventually a break with the Right-wing, as represented especially by Bukharin and Rykov, its chief spokesmen, and in the trade unions by Tomsky. Already at the 15th Party Congress in December 1927 Stalin had sounded the new emphasis. After pointing out that 'in the countryside,' by contrast with industry, 'we have a relatively slow growth of output,' he defined the twin tasks of the coming period as follows. *Firstly*, 'to maintain the achieved rate of development of socialist industry and to increase it in the near future with the object of creating conditions necessary for overtaking and surpassing the advanced capitalist countries.' 'The keynote of the development of our national economy,' he added, 'is *industrialisation* of the country, the increasingly important role of industry in relation to agriculture [...] an increase in the relative importance and commanding role of the socialist forms of economy.' *Secondly*, as regards agriculture, 'the way out is to turn the small and scattered peasant farms into large united farms based on cultivation of land in common, to go over to collective cultivation of the land on the basis of a new and higher technique. The way out is to unite the small and dwarf farms gradually but surely, not by pressure, but by example and persuasion, into large farms based on common, cooperative, collective cultivation of the land.' To this declaration he added the solemn words: 'There is no other way out.'[41]

The Congress resolved on an expansion of collective farming and the allocation of substantial capital investment to the creation of large-scale State farms, especially in Siberia, with the intention that by the end of the quinquennium these should contribute 150 million poods of grain for the market, or between one-half and two-thirds of what landlord estates had formerly done.[42]

For the time being, however, there was considerable caution in applying this new policy. The reference in Stalin's 15th Congress speech to 'gradually' and 'by example and persuasion' is to be noted (what in retrospect were called 'excesses', in the shape of forcible collectivisation and deportation of resisters, did not come until later). Care was still taken to combine the 'new turn' with the old emphasis on encouraging the middle peasant. In addressing a meeting of Moscow Party functionaries in April, Stalin, while emphasising that 'we must employ every effort towards the development of large farms in the rural districts on the lines of collective or soviet economy, farms which will in fact be grain factories for the whole country,' was careful at the same time to say that 'we must give the middle peasant a certain perspective,' to point out that it was not *only* the *kulak* who was holding back grain from the market at the present time, and to characterise the 'special measures' taken in the spring to collect grain as containing 'undoubtedly a great number of exaggerations and transgressions'.[43] To the latter question he was to return three months later at a meeting of Party functionaries in Leningrad, when he spoke of the need 'immediately to abolish the practice of unlawful searches of peasant farms and all relapses into methods of requisitioning'. At the same time he advocated some rise in the official purchase-price for grain. At the November (1928) Plenum meeting of the Central Committee he was underlining the 'abnormal outdistancing of our grain production as compared with our industrial development, accompanied by an enormous increase in the demand for grain from the growing cities and industrial centres,' and insisting that it is 'not our duty to *reduce* the rate of development of grain production' – 'either we solve this problem or we fail and face the inevitable breach between the socialist town and the petit-bourgeois village.' This was coupled with a criticism of the Right-wing (at this time with Frumkin of the Commissariat of Finance as the main target: he had counselled caution as regards both the rate of investment and measures against *kulak* farming). Five months later his attack on the so-called 'Right-wing danger' was more outspoken and emphatic, and was moreover directed at Bukharin as chief theoretical exponent of the 'NEP-growing-into-socialism' line and as one who was 'living in the past'. Class struggle in the countryside was now in the air. It was now 'not *any* kind of alliance with the peasantry, but only *such an alliance* as is based on the struggle against the capitalist-elements of the peasantry'.[44] In December came Stalin's attack on theories of 'equilibrium' and of 'spontaneity' as applied to the process of industrialisation and of transition to socialism.[45] It was in this 'year of great change' (1929-30) that the targets for collectivisation were changed upwards, and those for State farms were doubled; so that at the 16th Party Congress in June 1930 Stalin was able to boast that by the end of the First Five Year Plan the State Grain Trust (which organised the new State farms) would have 'as large an area under grain as the whole of Argentine today'. It was also in the course of 1929-30 that the policy of 'sharpened class struggle in the village' was carried a crucial stage further to become a new offensive against the *kulak* (and one that in practice did not confine itself to them, properly defined) with the aim of 'eliminating the *kulak* as a class'.

Apart from such major policy-questions as those of which we have been speaking, economic discussions of the late 1920s were chiefly concerned with questions of planning – its extent, its apparatus and methods. Although Gosplan, the State Planning Commission, had been instituted early in the decade (as an expansion of Goelro, or the State Commission for Electrification, of

1920), it continued to have no more than an advisory role, and even after the inauguration of its so-called 'Control Figures' in 1925, it lacked any authority over the various government departments or Ministries to enforce its own views and directives (or even, it would seem, to obtain advance-information about their sectional programmes and intentions). For a number of years it was concerned mainly with 'partial plans' and *ad hoc* projects, such as transport reorganisation and economic regionalisation. Even when the 'Control Figures' had become an annual event, these were prevented from having much operative significance for some years by the jealous sectionalism of various departments and even more by basic policy-differences still to be resolved. For many years the Commissariat of Finance, for example, was the stronghold of relatively conservative, Right-wing views, while Gosplan leaned, at least, towards the views of the Left Opposition with its advocacy of accelerated industrialisation. Sokolnikov, for example, was openly scornful of Gosplan's first essay in 'Control Figures', and even of planning in general; the one-time President of the State Bank regarded planning as 'an encroachment on the independence of the financial organs'; and the Commissariat of Agriculture was inclined to treat miscalculation in grain collecting as the fault, not of *kulak* ill-will, but of unrealistic 'paper plans, too casually and hastily drawn up'.[46] Only after the 14th Party Congress of December 1925, with its emphasis on industrialisation as the line of future economic advance, did the authority of Gosplan, as at first the coordinator and later the originator of departmental plans, begin to grow. From 1926 onward it became increasingly concerned with successive drafts of a five-year 'perspective plan', and of annual operational plans geared thereto (of which the control figures were to be the initial set of targets, issued, in theory at least, in advance of the preparation of departmental plans; the final operational plan being a coordinated revision of the latter). One general issue that was to emerge from these debates over the role of planning in general and of Gosplan in particular was that between the so-called 'objective' and 'subjective' schools, later to develop into the two broad tendencies in planning that were designated the 'genetic' approach and the 'teleological'. The difference consisted fundamentally of two contrasted views (or emphases) as to the mode of functioning of a socialist economy – or at least of a mixed economy transitional thereto. How far was such an economy 'governed by economic laws', as descriptions of spontaneous 'elemental forces', to which economic policy must bow and which policy-makers must study and learn from? Or how far, on the contrary, were economic events the servants and instruments of State policy, which in such an economy, no longer based essentially on the market, postulated certain ends and could employ administrative instruments to carry these into effect? It was, of course, the old argument of human will *versus* objective circumstance conducted in a new setting. Thus when Sokolnikov depicted the 'peasant plan' as 'taking the field against Gosplan,' indicating that the former was the ultimate master, he was implying that objective market forces were more powerful than any set of policy-directives. A more extreme representative of this viewpoint was Kondratiev, who at one time advised planners to 'avoid the fetishism of precise calculations' and to 'bow before an understanding of those processes which are in actual motion in the economy [and] grasp the basic processes which confront us.' Trotsky, *per contra*, in enthusiastically welcoming the first Control Figures, had spoken of them as 'a dialectical combination of theoretical precision and practical caution,' and of 'calculation of objective conditions and trends with a subjective definition of the tasks of the State'.[47] Another writer in the Gosplan organ argued that it is only with the introduction of the subjective element that planning (as distinct from forecasting) really starts.

> Until a subject appears, possessing its own goals, that is to say striving to change objective factors, and having the will to change them, there exists no plan, and no talk of a plan is possible. From this standpoint no depiction of past historical trends, even if quite true, and no discovery of laws of development, even if they are exact laws, [...] can constitute a plan. [...] The existing situation, a subjective will resolved to change it, a general goal as accompaniment to that will – these are the prerequisites of a plan. [...] From the standpoint of the goal the plan is neither a research-project nor a prognosis; it represents the preliminary to an outline draft of a decision. The actual drawing up of the plan is accordingly an administrative task, not research.[48]

Smilga, as chairman of Gosplan, took a middle position. 'We meet quite a lot of pitfalls in our planning work,' he remarked. 'On the one hand, underestimating the objective trends of economic development causes the economic plan to be treated as something arbitrary and opportunities open to the State for planning to be overestimated. On the other hand, absence of any long-run perspective and of goals results in a submission to elemental tendencies and to opportunism in practical policy.' Warning against 'maximalism' in planning, he said: 'Some maximalists hold that the goals are the most important element in planning. Such persons usually represent a plan as the expression of intention. [...] So sharp an emphasis on the element of the goal derives from the assumption that in our economic system objective deterministic processes have mainly died out, or are dying out. Hence a greater place is given to free will than it can have in actuality.'

Among Soviet economists generally in the early revolutionary years (and Bukharin in his more 'Leftist' period was among them) the view prevailed that a socialist economy could dispense with commodity-production (i.e. production for the market) altogether, and that accordingly it was no longer subject to 'laws of political economy'. In so far as the New Economic Policy of 1920 had reintroduced the peasant market, this 'dying out' of market-relations and of economic laws was temporarily qualified by the need to make concessions to the peasantry and their demands – a necessity which the theory of 'primitive socialist accumulation' was designed to subordinate or overcome. The compulsions of the market were usually conceived of exclusively in terms of the peasant market, and hence as consequent upon the coexistence of State industry with individualist peasant agriculture. Apart from this, the influence of a consumers' retail market does not seem to have been thought of. It followed that with every advance along the road to industrialisation, and every consequential enlargement of the socialist sector of the economy, the objective necessity could be the more subordinated to policy-directives of the plan. It is interesting to note that it was to this question that Stalin was to return twenty years and more later (in 1943 and again in 1952) with the *ex cathedra* pronouncement that objective conditions, in the shape of the 'law of value', still operated in a socialist economy, and planning, although not automatically regulated by it, must at least take its influence into account.

Inside Gosplan in the closing years of the decade during the campaign against 'the Right-wing danger', the so-called 'genetic' tendency came to be associated with the views of the economist Groman, and to a less extent Bazarov, who had adopted a method of extrapolating past trends and relationships into the coming period as basis for plan estimates, and employed a set of so-called 'static and dynamic coefficients' as a frame-work for plan-making. This method in turn became identified with Bukharin's theory of equilibrium, especially with the latter's implications as to the necessary relationships between the growth of agricultural production and the growth of industry, and was denounced as tending to reduce planning to mere economic forecasting, or 'prognosis', of what would tend to happen in its absence, and of exerting a 'pessimistic' and 'minimalist' bias upon estimates of what was practicable. Bazarov had tended to stress the limiting influence exerted by the large degree of obsolescence (as well as backwardness) of existing plant and equipment, demanding expensive reconstruction if not complete scrapping and replacement; and he had been so ill-advised as to suggest the inevitability of a 'descending curve' of growth as industrialisation proceded.[49]

Evidently such an argument scarcely admits of any definitive answer, at any rate in any simple formulation; and it is likely to remain a difference of relative emphasis so long as human action, individual or collective, is one factor *inter alia* in shaping the outcome of events and future history is qualitatively different from the past. Any scientific principle or method of planning from its nature must inevitably exert a 'deterministic' bias, since it is concerned with conditioning factors and relations and with limits on the possible, derived from the generalising of past experience. Such generalisations can be valid only to some degree of approximation when applied to new situations. This, however, is no sufficient reason for failing to use them, since to know what have been found to be conditioning factors and limits on the possible is a necessary condition of any effective action, even when elements of the new and the unforeseen are known to be present. Unwillingness to be a slave to such methods or to admit them as more than a starting-point may be the reason why some planners have been known to remark that planning is and must remain 'an art rather than a science'. In the atmosphere of 1929-30, such considerations, and particularly emphasis on what was *new*, seem to have led to an indiscriminate rejection of methods that deserved a place as permanent elements of planning techniques and could have been developed with advantage: methods which have re-emerged from disfavour and obscurity only in fairly recent years.

One crucial planning method that was a product of the 1920s and did survive was the method of balances. This consisted of the use of a series of particular balances of available supply of and current uses for particular commodities or commodity groups, which were used to test the internal consistency of any given plan. They were a flexible instrument, enabling plans to be worked and reworked, with allowance, moreover, for changing coefficients of output or use, and without any presumption that the two sides of the balance must be brought into equality by an adjustment of one side rather than the other. Thus if estimates were adjusted or conditions changed, a new balance could be achieved *either* by altering the output or by altering the uses of the item in question: e.g. if the demands for, say, coal or for steel proved to have been underestimated in the first draft of a plan, subsequent adjustment could be made either by raising the output-targets for coal-mining or steel-production or by pruning and rationing certain of the demands for coal or steel, by scaling down the output-targets for some using-industries or (more probably) by compelling them to adopt economy-measures or to resort to substitutes. Moreover, in the course of revising plans *some* balances could be re-worked in this fashion without the necessity of re-working the whole set or system of balance-relations. This could represent a considerable simplification and saving of time (a major consideration, especially in constructing annual operational plans, which were often late in completion); and might well result in a sufficiently good approximation in the given conditions, where some margin of error in the estimating was inevitable. But this very advantage of simplicity and flexibility concealed a potential disadvantage. It represented a device that operated essentially in terms of a series of isolated *partial* equilibria; it was not a system of *general* equilibrium; and there were occasions when the repercussions (implicit but not explicit) upon other sets of outputs and inputs that were ignored in the course of readjustment could amount in the aggregate to a considerable magnitude – a magnitude larger than could be contained within the limits of tolerance set by the practical requirements of attaining a given degree of approximation. Thus it became common planning practice, in making adjustments, only to take account of so-called 'linkages' or effects that were immediately related to any given change of output or input, and to ignore more remote 'linkages' or effects. In some cases this might involve serious inconsistencies at other points of the plan – inconsistencies involving in practice various strains and wastage of productive resources. Not only this, but the method *per se* provided no criterion for ensuring that any plan adopted yielded the maximum result for the economy as a whole (in the sense of maximising gross production, aggregated in some way, or alternatively producing a *given* output total with the minimum expenditure of productive resources). As Professor Oskar Lange has put the problem in theoretical terms:

> The second part of programming consists in the establishment of the optimum set of means to be used, i.e. a set of means leading to the maximum realisation of the end. This is called the choice of the optimum programme. The optimum programme is chosen only from internally consistent programmes, since internally inconsistent programmes cannot be carried out in practice. As a rule there is a large (most frequently an infinite) number of internally consistent programmes from which the choice of the optimum programme is made.[50]

The balance-method was devised in the middle 1920s in parallel with the preparation of the first Control Figures; and it was this that caught the attention of Leontief at the time and formed the germ of the more generalised and sophisticated input-output system, developed later by Leontief himself. Its development along these lines was apparently ignored in the Soviet Union, partly perhaps for the reasons mentioned in the last paragraph and partly because the devisers of such general systems of coefficients and of the notions of equilibrium-relations in development alike fell under criticism in the bitter discussions of 1929-30.

Towards the end of the decade of the 1920s, alongside discussion of the Five Year Plan, the attention of Gosplan was also devoted to various long-term plans (extending over periods of 10 or 15 years). In connection with this there was some theoretical work on what would today be termed 'mathematical models', the most interesting of which was the work of Feldman. This was of special interest in that it attempted to develop Marx's famous schema of reproduction in a dynamic sense: in addition to assigning a key importance to the notion of a capital-output-ratio, he analysed the effect of various allocations of investment between Marx's two departments or sectors (capital goods production and consumer goods production) upon the general growth-rate, including the growth-rate of consumption at various dates within the planning period.[51]

Feldman had the distinction of so adapting Marx's two-sector-model as to separate out those activities (within Marx's Department I) which were exclusively concerned with new investment, and hence with growth, from all those (including the supply of means of production for current replacement) which were involved in maintaining the current flow of consumer goods. This, he claimed, was necessary (as, indeed, it is in one form or another) to complete their adaptation to the circumstances of 'expanded reproduction' (by contrast with the static case of 'simple reproduction' to which Marx had initially applied his Schema). He then shows that the future growth-rate of the system (including the future growth-rate of consumption) depends essentially on how the output of the former sector (the investment sector) is allocated *between* the two sectors – i.e. allocated for the expansion of the investment sector and of the consumption sector respectively.[52] On this allocation will depend the relative productive capacities of the sectors (measured by their capital equipment) at future dates; and on the relative size of the former sector will depend the capacity of the economy to grow. Hence for any given desired growth-rate of consumption (e.g. some constant geometric rate) there was, *ceteris paribus*, a certain relationship between the capital of these two sectors. Such a relationship he took as an index of 'the level of industrialisation'.

This analysis served in effect as a justification of priority of development for heavy industry (since this would raise the 'level of industrialisation' and hence the potential growth-rate), at any rate if attention was focussed upon changes in consumption levels in the second decade, rather than in the early years of the first.[53] It was also one kind of answer to Bazarov's 'descending curve' of growth, in the sense that this could be turned into a constant, or even increasing, growth-rate (for some quinquennia at least) by assigning sufficient investment-priority to the investment-sector of Marx's Department I.

Unfortunately work along these lines was also to be discontinued, perhaps for the same, or analogous, reasons as those we have mentioned in connection with the method of input-output balances. Such attempts, it seems, came to be regarded as barren formalism. Kuibyshev, when recently appointed to the chairmanship of Gosplan, in the early '30s spoke derogatively of the 'statistical-arithmetical deviation in planning', and appealed for greater realism, more attention to practice and less theory. This statement was even quoted approvingly by a chairman of Gosplan as late as 1956.[54] The subsequent revival of interest in mathematical methods in economic analysis and in planning (especially in conjunction with computer-programming techniques) has brought renewed attention to mathematical models as applied to development. At the same time a place of increasing importance has been assigned to long-term planning. This, together with emphasis on the better use of capital equipment in industry and on calculating the time-factor in the allocation and employment of investible resources, has encouraged a new attention to the notion of an 'optimum' in planning, and the use of 'linear programming' tools to this end.

NOTES

1. E.H. Carr, *The Bolshevik Revolution 1917-1923*, London, 1952. Vol. 2, pp3-10. Rudolph Schlesinger, *Marx, his Time and Ours*, London, 1950, pp353 seq.
2. Cf. the well-known Preface of Marx and Engels to the Russian edition of *The Communist Manifesto* of January 1882; also Letter of Marx to the Editor of *Otye-chestvennie Zapiski*, 1877; of Engels to Vera Zasulich, 23 April 1885, and to Danielson, 24 Feb. 1893 and 17 Oct. 1893.
3. One of the earliest decrees nationalising a particular enterprise (that of Sovnarcom, 20 Dec. 1917) applied to a mining company whose management was alleged to have 'refused to submit to the decree on workers' control over production'.
4. For this period cf. the present writer's *Soviet Economic Development since 1917*, London, 1948, Chapter 4; E.H. Carr, *op. cit.*, Vol. 2, Chap. XVI.
5. Lenin later (March 1919) spoke of the revolution as being mainly a bourgeois revolution up to the summer or even autumn of 1918.

6. E.H. Carr, *op. cit.*, p261.
7. Speech on the Food Tax, April 21st, 1921.
8. Speech on NEP, reported in *Izvestia*, Oct. 19, 1921; *cit.* by the present author in *Soviet Economic Development*, *p*123.
9. At the Congress Stalin spoke of 'the conversion of our country from an agrarian into an industrial country able to produce the machinery it needs by its own efforts -that is the essence, the basis of our general line'; and the resolution of the Congress declared: 'In the sphere of economic development the Congress holds that in our land, the land of the dictatorship of the proletariat, there is 'every requisite for the building of a complete socialist society' (Lenin). The Congress considers that the main task of our Party is to fight for the victory of socialist construction in the U.S.S.R.'
10. Alexander Erlich, *The Soviet Industrialisation Debate, 1924-1928*, Harvard, 1960.
11. In the Preface to *1905* (Russian ed. 1922, pp4-5) Trotsky went so far as to say that following its seizure of power the proletariat would 'come into conflict, not only with all bourgeois groups which had supported it during the first period of revolutionary struggle, but with the broad masses of the peasantry who had helped it to seize power. The contradictions of a situation of a workers' government in a country with a preponderantly peasant population can only find their solution [...] on the battlefield of world proletarian revolution.' In his Preface to the re-issue in 1919 (in Moscow) of his *A Review and Some Perspectives* (as it was entitled in the English version of 1921, published in Moscow by the Comintern) he wrote: 'Once in power, the proletariat not only will not want, but will not be able to limit itself to a bourgeois democratic programme. It will be able to carry through the Revolution to the end only in the event of the Russian Revolution being converted into a Revolution of the European proletariat. [...] Therefore, once having won power, the proletariat cannot keep within the limits of bourgeois democracy. It must adopt the tactics of *permanent revolution*, i.e. [...] go over to more and more radical social reforms and seek direct and immediate support in revolution in Western Europe.'
12. E.H. Carr, *op. cit.*, Vol. 4 (*The Interregnum 1923-1924*), pp92-9, 107-120; M. H. Dobb, *op. cit.*, pp161-176.
13. E.H. Carr, *op. cit.*, Vol. 4, pp21-2.
14. Among the immediate reforms proposed in this report were: to

afford to the peasantry the alternative of paying the existing agricultural tax in cash or in kind, and to substitute a *single* agricultural tax for all existing taxes on the peasantry.

15. Letter to the Central Committee of the Party of October 8, 1923. The reference to financial policy presumably had the credit-restriction of recent months in mind.
16. Articles in *Pravda* reprinted early in 1924 as *Novy Kurs*, pp70-1.
17. Mention was also made of failure to carry out the programme of grain export owing to difficulties in purchasing grain. The text of this *Declaration* is printed as an Appendix to Vol. 4 of E.H. Carr, *op. cit.*
18. The phrase, indeed, was Trotsky's, who had written (in *Novy Kurs*): 'I have had occasion to say that the "dictatorship" ought to belong, not to finance, but to industry [...]. Not only foreign trade, but also the re-establishing of a stable currency ought to be strictly subordinated to the interests of State industry.'
19. Later in his *Novaia Ekonomika* he was at pains to argue that 'the possibilities of rationalising production within the frame of the old technique approaches exhaustion', and hence the possibility of more intensive use of existing capital equipment was small. Reconstruction (on the basis of higher organic composition of capital) of existing plants or construction of new ones was accordingly essential.
20. E. Preobrazhensky, in *Vestnik Komm. Akademia*, Vol. VIII (1924), pp59 seq.
21. This was summarised in the present writer's *Russian Economic Development since the Revolution* (London, 1928), pp259-262; also in his *Soviet Economic Development since 1917* (London, 1948), pp183-5.
22. See, for example, A. Erlich, *op. cit.*, pp32-59 and *passim.*
23. Isaac Deutscher, for example, refers to his 'scholar's utter indifference to tactics' (*The Prophet Unarmed*, London, 1959, p237).
24. *Cit.* A. Erlich, *op. cit.*, p37. This *political* setting and preoccupation of the economic reasoning of the time is something that Dr Erlich ignores. On this cf. also I Deutscher, *The Prophet Unarmed*, pp234-8, and *The Prophet Outcast* (London, 1963), pp108-9.
25. Article, *A New Revelation about Soviet Economics, or How to Destroy the Worker-Peasant Alliance*, first printed in *Pravda*, Dec. 12, 1924; later reprinted as *Kritika Ekonomicheskoi Platformy Oppozitsii* (Moscow, 1926); English translation in *International Press Correspondence*, 20 Jan, 1925 (Vol. 5, No. 5), pp39-48.

26. In a Speech to Party Functionaries of Leningrad on 28 July 1926.
27. English translation as *The Party and the Opposition Bloc, Part II*, in *International Press Correspondence*, Vol. 6, No. 58, p980 (26 August 1926).
28. For some details of these measures, cf. the present writer's *Russian Economic Development since the Revolution*, pp345-150; E.H. Carr, *op. cit.*, pp249 seq.
29. The slogan of 'Face to the Village' had dated from an article by Zinoviev in *Pravda* of 30 July 1924; with the keynote statement: 'It is high time to oblige a number of our organisations *to turn their face more to the countryside.*'
30. Cf. for the higher figure I. Deutscher, *op. cit.*, p233 footnote.
31. Rykov at the 15th Party Conference in 1926 quoted figures for 1925 to show that some 3.3 per cent of all peasant holdings were larger than 10 dessiatines (= *approximately* 10 hectares), and 3 per cent owned more than 4 head of cattle. Holdings of 6 dessiatines and more composed 13.5 per cent of all holdings. At the same time between 4 and 5 per cent of peasants were without land and one-third had holdings of less than 2 dessiatines. As regards liability to Agricultural Tax, it was pointed out at the time that 15 per cent of the peasantry paid 40 per cent of the tax, while 25 per cent of peasants (the poorest) were exempt (figures cited by A. Martynov in *Communist International* (Eng. edition), Nov. 30th. 1926, p9.
32. One can say, I think, that a fairly consistent Centre-position of this kind was maintained in these years by Stalin.
33. In a speech of 17 April 1925, just before the 14th Party Conference, published in *Pravda* of *24* April.
34. *Cit.* Deutscher, *op. cit.*, p240.
35. L. Shanin in *Bolshevik*, 1926, No. 2, pp.70 seq.; *Ekonomicheskoe Obozrenie*, Nov. 1925, pp25 seq.
36. *Cit.* E.H. Carr, *Socialism in One Country*, Vol. I, pp335-6, 351. At the 14th Party Congress he had also spoken of the necessity for stimulating agricultural exports in order to finance the import of equipment and raw materials for industry; but he had been criticised by Stalin for wishing to give priority to light industry over heavy ('if we remain at this stage of development in which we do not ourselves manufacture the means of production, but have to import them, we cannot have any safeguard against the transformation of our country into an appendage of the capitalist system' – Stalin's reply to the discussion at the 14th Congress).

37. Cf. *Kontrolnie Tsifri 1927-8*; also 2nd edition (1928) of the present writer's *Russian Economic Development since the Revolution*, Appendix, pp416-428.
38. Cf. Rykov's report to the Plenum of the Central Committee on 24 Nov. 1928 (there are approximately 62 poods in one ton).
39. Rykov told the 15th Party Congress that total peasant grain sales (i.e. including the private market) in the past five months 'scarcely exceeded the level of 1925'.
40. Rykov stated (in his report to the 15th Party Congress) that in the final quarter of 1927 wage-funds in State industry increased by 10 per cent and peasant incomes by 30 per cent.
41. J. Stalin, *Works*, Eng. edition, Vol. 10 pp303, 310-12; *Pravda*, Dec. 6 and 9, 1927. The 15th Congress, in addition to considering a draft of the First Five Year Plan, agreed upon 'a series of new measures for the purpose of restricting the development of capitalism in the village and of guiding peasant farms in the direction of socialism'.
42. The First Five Year Plan, in its original form, only envisaged that a quarter of peasant households and some 15 per cent of cultivated area would be in collective farms by 1933 (cf. the writer's *Soviet Economic Development since 1917*, pp224-5).
43. Moscow meeting of 13 April 1928.
44. J. Stalin, *Leninism*, 1940, Eng. edition, p240.
45. *Ibid.*, p306. The reference was largely to Bukharin's *Notes of an Economist* in which the dangers of a rupture of equilibrium between industry and agriculture and between different industrial sectors were emphasised, with the implication that the rate of investment and of growth was being unduly forced *(inter alia*, Bukharin here used the term 'dynamic economic equilibrium'.)
46. Cf. E.H. Carr, *Socialism in One Country*, Vol. I, pp506-7.
47. *Towards Socialism or Capitalism?*, first published in *Pravda*, 20 Sept. 1925; cit. E.H. Carr, *ibid.*, p505.
48. S. Sharov, in *Planovoe Khoziaistvo*, 1926, No. 7, pp59 seq.
49. Cf. the writer's *Soviet Economic Development since 1917*, pp327-31. In the fevered atmosphere of 1929-30 Bazarov was for this denounced and charged as a 'wrecker'. It is interesting, if somewhat unpleasant, to read today the mathematician Boiarski, in recent years a strong critic of Kantorovitch and of 'bourgeois econometrics', at that time denouncing Bazarov and his 'descending curve' as 'theoretical sabotage' (in *Planovoe Khoziaistvo*, 1930, Nos. 10-11).

Bazarov is twitted in this article on his 'Machism'; and reference is made to 'ideological fight against those arrested by the G.P.U'. as well as against 'enemies still at large'.

50. *Political Economy*, Vol. I, Eng. edition, Warsaw and Oxford, 1963, pp194-5.
51. G. A. Feldman in *Planovoe Khoziaistvo*, 1928, Nos. 11 and 12 (Nov. and Dec.), 1929, No. 12 (Dec). In one place Feldman uses an equation which is virtually identical with the well-known (but later) growth-equation of Harrod *(Planovoe Khoziaistvo*, Dec. 1929. No. 12, p116).
52. Feldman incidentally uses the notion of 'effectiveness of capital' (defining it as the ratio of the net output of a period to the total capital employed, both output and capital being valued in terms of current cost of reproduction); and he also emphasises that a rising 'organic composition of capital' need not imply a fall in 'effectiveness of capital'.
53. Cf. E. D. Domar, *Essays on the Theory of Economic Growth* (New York, 1957), pp223 seq. and the present writer's *Essay on Economic Growth and Planning*, (London, 1960), pp72-3.
54. *Cit.* G. Sorokin, *Planovoe Khoziaistvo*, 1956, No. 1, p43. Feldman's analysis had unfortunately been used by some of his associates in Gosplan in support of some over-optimistic long-term plan-forecasts in 1930, and had been dismissed with the latter as abstract and unrealistic.

Planning

The general idea of economic planning is usually attributed to, and associated with, nineteenth century pioneers of socialist thought. It was rather natural to suppose that something of the kind would have to replace the market mechanism which the Classical Economists had demonstrated as the self-acting regulator of an atomistic society of individual enterprise – Adam Smith's famous 'unseen hand' of economic laws operating through the medium of free competition (a medium which bent and subordinated individual interest to serve social ends). Actually the pioneers of socialist thought said remarkably little on the subject. Saint-Simon had merely spoken of the future society being 'organised according to general forethought'; and Professor Landauer, in his historical work on *European Socialism*, has said: 'Forethought is the essence of planning. For the rest of the nineteenth century, and for the first part of the twentieth, the idea of planning was entirely overshadowed in the minds of socialists by the postulate of more equitable distribution. Yet, the roots of modern concepts of planning go back to the teachings of the Saint-Simonians'. With Marx and his colleague Engels reference to planning was more explicit; but omission of any detail concerning it was intentional, since they were keen to renounce the approach of those they termed 'utopian socialists', and believed that it was idle to try to sketch more than the general outlines of a future stage of society until at least the threshold of such a new stage had been reached, historically speaking, and until one was in a position to obtain some concrete picture of what its foundations and its real (as distinct from imagined) problems would look like. Apart from a few general statements about planning of the distribution of productive labour by society replacing the spontaneous operation of market forces, nothing was specifically said as to how this was envisaged as operating, in what kind of institutions it was to be embodied, how centralised or decentralised it might possibly be. (Engels in *Socialism, Utopian and Scientific* had referred to 'socialised production according to a predetermined plan' and in *Anti-Duhring* to 'anarchy of social production' being replaced by 'conscious organisation of society on the basis of a plan'; while Marx himself, in Volume III of *Capital*, referred, quite incidentally, to producers 'regulat[ing] their production according to a preconceived plan', to 'society organised as a conscious and systematic association', establishing 'a direct relation between the quantities of social labour time employed in the production of particular articles and the quantity of the demand of society for them'; but that was all).

THEORETICAL DEBATE

When critics of socialism among economists on the continent of Europe, like Professors Halm, Pierson and von Mises, early in the twentieth century developed the beginnings of a theoretical criticism of such an economic order, they assumed unquestioningly that economic planning with a high degree of centralised decision-taking would inevitably characterise a society with publicly-owned means of production; treating it as axiomatic that such planning would replace entirely the market mechanism (except possibly in the case of things sold retail to individual consumers), and that if the State owned industry it would necessarily decree what industry did by the procedure of issuing detailed orders in some form to its leading and subordinate employees (as with any State organ or department). The economists' attack on planning, and particularly that of von Mises, took the form of contending that, in the absence of a market, such a system would lack any criterion of rationality, and hence would have no way of distinguishing an 'economic' allocation of resources or method of production from an uneconomic one. For this reason the debate was commonly referred to as that about *wirtschaftsrechnung* – as to whether rational economic calculation was possible at all. Von Mises wrote in his well-known article in the *Archiv für Sozialwissenschaften* Vol. XLVII, April 1920:

> The significance of Money in a society where the means of production are State-controlled will be different from that which

> attaches to it in one where they are privately owned. It will be, in fact, incomparably narrower ... inasmuch as it will be confined to consumption goods. Moreover, just because no production good will ever become the object of exchange, it will be impossible to determine its monetary value. Money could never fill in a socialist state the role it fills in a competitive society in determining the value of production-goods. Calculation in terms of money will here be impossible.
>
> It is precisely in market dealings that market prices to be taken as the basis of calculation are formed for all kinds of goods and labour employed. Where there is no free market, there is no pricing mechanism; without a pricing mechanism, there is no economic calculation.

Earlier (in a well-known article in the *Giornale degli Economisti* of 1908) Enrico Barone as a disciple of Pareto had examined the conditions which the Ministry of Production in a Collectivist State would have to observe 'to achieve the maximum advantage from its operations', and concluded that 'the system of equations of collectivist equilibrium are no other than that of free competition'. He affirmed 'the impossibility of solving such equations *a priori*'; and declared in summary 'how fantastic those doctrines are which imagine that production in the collectivist regime would be ordered in a manner substantially different from that of "anarchist" production'.

In the course of the 1930s the challenge was taken up by a number of socialist economists, most notably by Professor H.D. Dickinson in England and by Professor Oskar Lange of Poland (at the time of writing in the United States). The answer of the former has been termed the 'competitive solution' since it sought to demonstrate, in effect, that public ownership of land and capital was by no means inconsistent with the preservation of a market for so-called 'factors of production' (or 'producers' goods') and the existence of competition between State enterprises in sale and purchase. Professor Oskar Lange did not appeal to actual markets for a solution, but relied instead (although somewhat analogously) upon a system of 'accounting prices' on the basis of which productive decisions could be taken; these 'accounting prices' being varied in accordance with the prevailing relationship between supply and demand in the case of the goods or productive 'factors' in question. Thus, for example, the central authority in offering loan- or investment-funds for hire by industrial boards or enterprises would fix a loan-price or interest-rate for their use; this would be raised if applications exceeded the total investment-fund available, and lowered in the converse case. He refers to a 'trial and error procedure in a socialist economy'. Professor Lange summed-up his answer to von Mises in these terms:

> Professor Mises' contention that a socialist economy cannot solve the problem of rational allocation of its resources is based on a confusion concerning the nature of prices ... The term 'price' has two meanings. It may mean either price in the ordinary sense, i.e. the exchange ratio of two commodities on a market, or it may have the generalised meaning of 'terms on which alternatives are offered' ... It is only prices in the generalised sense which is indispensable to solving the problem of allocation of resources ... But Professor Mises seems to have confused prices in the narrower sense, i.e., the exchange ratios of commodities on a market, with prices in the wider sense of 'terms on which alternatives are offered' (*On the Economic Theory of Socialism*, University of Minnesota, 1938, pp59-61).

Those who had previously upheld the position that solution of the problem was theoretically inconceivable in a socialist economy now shifted their position to one of affirming that, while conceivable, and not to be excluded *a priori*, its successful solution in practice was highly improbable (Lange spoke of this as 'a second line of defence' of the Mises-position). Reference was made to the thousands, indeed millions, of equations that a planning body would have to solve. This was the position taken by Professor Hayek and Professor Robbins; the latter of whom said that while 'on paper we can conceive this problem to be solved by a series of mathematical calculations ... in practice this solution is quite unworkable' (L. Robbins, *The Great Depression*, London, 1934, p151). The force of this contention can be said to have been greatly weakened since then by the invention of the electronic computer, together with linear programming techniques for the solution of optimising and allocation problems. Even so, there would still be those who would contend that practical obstacles to successful computation make it highly unlikely that planned decision-making will reach more than a very low degree of 'optimising' or even attain any high degree of internal consistency in its plans. This matter of feasibility is evidently relevant to the question of how much detail can be included in centralised decision-taking (itself dependent, not only on efficient computation, but also upon possession of reliable information in an appropriate form) – a question to which we shall return.

In this connection it is to be noticed that, not only Dickinson's 'competitive solution', but also the 'accounting prices' method suggested by Lange, afford an answer to the problem by proposing a highly decentralised mechanism of decision-taking, and reducing centralised decision-taking at top-levels to a minimum. Thus they assert that such a mechanism is not inconsistent with social or public ownership of means of production, and that it is capable of practical operation. What they were essentially doing was to propose the combination of social ownership with some kind of market, or else quasi-market, mechanism; they did *not* contend as against von Mises that a solution was possible consistently with centralised planning *per se*. There were some who contended for the latter even in the discussions of the '30s. For example, Robert Hall, the author of *The Economic System in a Socialist State* (London, 1937) maintained that since 'demand for the factors of production is a derived demand ... there is no theoretical difficulty in the way of calculating costs ... so long as there is a market in consumers' goods'. But since allocation of capital must in practice consist of the allocation in the case of each individual capital good *sui generis* (type of metal or fuel, type of machine tool), the problem is distinctly more cumbrous than at first sight might appear, and to such allocation the method of costing and pricing of each such item is, of course, crucial.

'INDICATIVE PLANNING' UNDER CAPITALISM

In more recent times the notion of 'planning' has been associated no longer exclusively with social ownership of the means of production. After the Second World War it began to be talked about, and even to some extent applied, in capitalist countries also. To a large extent this was a result of war-time experience of government controls and 'steering the economy' (also of rationing of supplies both among firms and among individual consumers) and represented a deliberate attempt to extend such methods into peace-time to deal with problems of the post-war epoch. Discussion of planning was also stimulated by attention to the problems of underdeveloped countries, in connection with international schemes of economic aid, sponsored by the United Nations, World Bank etc.

In France in 1947 there was the so-called Monnet Plan. In the ensuing years plans were drawn up for periods of four to five years in Netherlands and Scandinavia and Belgium. In Italy there was the Vanoni Plan; even in Britain some years later there was a so-called National Plan, which was no more than a forecast on paper and had little or no operative significance. For purposes of clarity of distinction, some people would prefer to speak of all this as 'programming' rather than 'planning'. The term 'indicative planning' was, indeed, used at the time to refer to this kind of somewhat tentative capitalist planning or 'steering'. Evidently it makes all the difference, especially where implementation is concerned, whether this is applied to socially owned enterprises and to a public sector or to autonomous private business concerns. The latter cannot be 'directed' or coerced save in exceptional circumstances (e.g. in time of war) or by exceptional methods (and then these methods are likely to be resisted and evaded). The theoretical explanation of such 'indicative planning', used to exhibit its specific effect, has been, however, that the plans, on the contrary to having an obligatory character, will serve as 'guide-lines' of future development, which to the extent that they are *expected* to be followed, even approximately, will introduce a measure of coordination between sectors and industries, facilitating long-term investment-decisions which might otherwise fail to be made. How successful such 'steering' could be depended in the main on how far individual firms expected that others would be influenced in their decisions by the indicated targets or, on the contrary, would ignore them. Some, however, have gone beyond the idea of a plan as mere guide-lines for private enterprise to take or leave as they please, and have interpreted 'indicative planning' as a bringing together of the large firms and groups and encouraging them 'to conclude a series of *bargains* about their future behaviour, which will have the effect of moving economic events along the desired path'.

RECENT DISCUSSION

Later, in the post-war period, the focus of discussion about planning shifted in two important respects: greater attention was devoted to the importance of income-distribution as qualifying propositions about 'efficiency' conditions in the allocation of economic resources, and interest shifted from conditions of static equilibrium to economic growth.

Firstly, regarding distribution: a greater emphasis upon this at later stages of discussion severely qualified the attempts of economic theory to justify the market system (given competition) on the grounds of its 'automatic' fulfilment of 'efficiency conditions' which a planned economy was, allegedly, incapable of doing. Already in a work such as Pigou's *Economics of Welfare* the distribution of income was stressed as one of the two main conditions affecting the maximisation of economic welfare (the implication being that it could only be maximised if distribution was altered in the direction of equality). Nonetheless, he sought to propound certain efficiency-conditions for maximising national income (or total net product) despite the fact that from a welfare (or utility) point of view such 'maximising' was entirely relative to distribution (because the addition to utility of an additional unit of a product depends entirely on whether it is consumed by someone of high income or by someone of low income). True, from the late '30s onwards a writer such as Prof. Lionel Robbins in England, and more widely among American economists, sought to banish questions of distribution by reverting to Pareto's 'denial of the possibility of interpersonal comparisons of utility' and, with a positivist emphasis, affirming that economics as a positive and *wertfrei* science must confine itself to the propounding of theorems about 'efficiency', in the sense of maximising production. But considerations about income-distribution could not be banished as easily as this; and it was soon to become clear that, if the denial of interpersonal comparisons was rigorously adhered to, nothing could be propounded about maximising production as a total (since the summation of heterogeneous product into a total was implicitly done in terms of utility – which prices were assumed to reflect or measure – and any such summation was accordingly relative to distribution). The so-called 'compensation principle' was devised to surmount this difficulty and to enable 'efficiency' conditions to be propounded even though 'interpersonal comparisons' were barred. But the outcome of an intricate and long-drawn-out debate in the '50s was to show that such a principle could not be enunciated without involving contradiction – contradiction due once more to the intrusion of the influence of income-distribution which had been supposedly 'banished'.

It accordingly followed that, if 'efficiency' judged from the standpoint of social welfare was necessarily relative to income-distribution and there was no reason to suppose that the income-distribution created by the market bore any relation to the 'ideal', the 'efficiency' of a free market system could be seen to be no more than an *approximation* to the maximum at best. Some, viewing large income-inequalities and the imperfections of competition, would claim that such 'efficiency' was distinctly low. Even if a planned economy were to fall a long way short of attaining the 'optimum conditions for efficiency' that economists sought to emphasise, it by no means necessarily followed that planning was inferior to a market system.

Secondly, we come to the shift in the focus of economic discussion from static equilibrium to dynamics after the Second World War, and the relation of this to the debate about planning. This new interest in economic growth as the central issue arose partly out of the relatively neglected (pre-1930) study of business cycles, partly (arising therefrom) interest in rates of growth and in the long-term trend. One thing to emerge from this discussion was the high degree of instability attending economic growth, not only as regards its tendency to fluctuations, but also the possibility of divergent rather than convergent movement with respect to any equilibrium trend. The key to growth and development is, of course, capital accumulation or investment, and hence the activities of the capital goods sector of industry. Investment in an atomistic free market economy is subject to a double uncertainty: uncertainty in the nature of things about factors affecting the long-term trend (such as technical progress, changes in tastes, demographic shifts and the like), and also uncertainty about the intentions and actions of other firms in the same industry and of other industries – actions which are themselves going to determine the near-future trend of prices and profitability. For example, whether expansion of the capital goods sector is profitable or not will depend on the future investment trend in general – whether this is likely to decline or to increase or to remain roughly constant. Yet this is one of the unknowns in an unplanned free market economy of the kind that Mises and his school extolled for its 'automaticity'. The result of this attention to growth was thus to emphasise the potential advantage of planning in moderating, or even possibly eliminating, the pronounced fluctuations to which economic growth had hitherto been subject, thus importing stability into development, and also increasing the rate of growth by reducing uncertainty about the nature of the long-term trend.

SOVIET PLANNING

It has been the Soviet Union, however, where economic planning has been carried to its furthest extent, and with which the term has come to be primarily associated. It is the Soviet Union (and nowadays other socialist countries of Eastern Europe) to which attention is usually paid when seeking for the lessons that experience has afforded – experience which has now extended over four decades in what has been quite a variety of circumstances. Since the end of the Second World War a number of other countries of Eastern and South-Eastern Europe have similarly adopted centralised planning, closely patterned, in the early years at least, on the Soviet type even to a mechanical extent. The exception to this has been Yugoslavia, which after an initial few years, following the war, of centralised planning on the Soviet model, carried out a sweeping decentralisation in 1951-2 (following her political break with the Soviet Union) and adopted something resembling the kind of decentralised 'model' of a socialist economy suggested in the economists' debate of the 1930s of which we have spoken.

Although the origin of a planning commission in the Soviet case dates from the end of the Civil War in 1921 (the famous Gosplan which grew out of the State Commission for Electrification of the previous year), effective planning did not really start until the end of the decade of the '20s with the launching of the First Five Year Plan. In its early years Gosplan was concerned with nothing more comprehensive than partial plans for special 'key' sectors of economic activity which had suffered severely in the Civil War and whose reconstruction was urgent for the restoration of production at large: such things as a transport plan, a fuel plan and so forth. Control and coordination of industry, meanwhile, was the function of special Commissariats (or Ministerial departments) coordinated by the Supreme Council of National Economy (*Vesenha*). Agriculture at the time consisted of some 25 million small peasant holdings, with no more than a comparative handful of large State farms, and was being wooed back to normal production by the provisions of the New Economic Policy (which had as its cornerstone the peasants' right to free trading in agricultural produce subject to the payment of an agricultural tax to the State). While private trade was quite legal at this period, the bulk of trade in agricultural produce between town and country was in the hands of State trading bodies and Cooperatives. So far as industry was concerned at this period the tendency was towards decentralisation and production for the market. The war-time regime of centralised allocation of supplies to factories and of direct collection of their production quotas by State bodies was terminated, and industrial enterprises (for the most part of the period termed industrial Trusts, as groupings of production plants or factories) were permitted, indeed obliged, to procure their supplies of raw materials, components, fuel and power etc., by direct contractual relations with suppliers, and similarly to dispose of their output to prospective buyers and procurers. The principle of *Khozraschot* (economic accounting on the basis of an autonomous balance sheet) was affirmed as the ruling principle of economic activity. Coupled with this, the individual responsibility of the manager of a factory or enterprise (who was appointed not elected) was also made into a ruling principle. Emphasis was also laid on the distinction between 'general direction and control (steering)' as the province of higher bodies and 'detailed operation and execution' of general policy-objectives.

Gosplan's first, and still tentative, essay in comprehensive industrial planning was the famous Control Figures for 1925-6 (comprised in a slender volume of no more than 100 pages). These represented a first attempt at drafting an annual production plan. They were designed as 'guide-lines' (*orientovka*) for the various Commissariats to take into account in constructing their own sectional programmes, but they did not have the character of obligatory directives. In presenting them to the Government, Gosplan in fact described them as 'a*pproximate* directives for the work of formulating actual operational plans'. In practice, however, they seem to have been largely ignored by the various departments responsible for actual programmes. In subsequent years, however, efforts were made to improve the statistical information upon which forecasting was based, while at the same time subordinate planning organs were instituted at lower levels of economic operation. Meanwhile the annual control figures gained both in extent and in the attention paid to them. In August 1927 a resolution of the Central Committee of the Party had called for them to be converted from 'general guiding lines' into 'concrete directives for the drafting of all operative plans'; and with the coming into operation of the First Five Year Plan (for the drafting of which special long-term-planning departments of Gosplan had been responsible) the Control Figures began to play a regular role, in the shape of so-called 'control limits', as the initial framework or draft for the construction of the detailed operative annual plan; this latter, in turn, being related to, and in theory built within, the longer-term 'perspective plan' covering five years.

The decade that was to follow the inauguration of the First Five Year Plan in 1928-9 had certain peculiarities that were to endow planning, and the problems confronting it, with some special features: features that in other circumstances might have been absent. In particular, both planning and economic administration became increasingly centralised as the decade advanced: centralised in the sense that more and more detail was included in the operational plans or else included in supplementary directives from the Ministries (as the former Commissariats came to be renamed); and the discretion and latitude allowed to lower levels, and in particular to the managements of industrial enterprises, were equivalently curtailed. This was in striking contrast to the pre-1928 situation. The launching of the First Five-Year Plan had been dominated by certain political aims (which had been the subject of acute controversy in the preceding years): namely, to achieve the industrialisation of the country within a short span of time; this achievement being dependent upon an extensive transformation of agriculture onto a collectivised basis (i.e. collective or cooperative farming in place of traditional individual and small-scale peasant farming). In retrospect this could be spoken of as 'a great leap'; and it was largely conceived, and certainly carried through, in terms of 'campaigns' and 'drives' and concentrations of available forces on this or that 'economic front' according to what happened to be the principal economic 'bottlenecks' in the situation at the time. The First Five Year Plan had been prepared originally in two variants, a minimal and a maximal; the latter resting on the most optimistic estimating of such factors as the foreign trade balance, harvests and agricultural deliveries, etc. It was the maximal variant that was finally adopted by the Government as the definitive plan; and in the course of its implementation the targets written into the annual plans, especially in the case of heavy industry, were revised sharply upwards under the slogan of 'Carry out the Five Year Plan in Four Years'.

An exceptionally high rate of growth was thus provided for, entailing an unprecedentedly high rate of construction and large structural changes in the economy, as well as large-scale transfers of labour (and hence population) from agriculture to industry. As the decade advanced, the growing war danger (following the rise of Hitler Fascism, combined in the Far East with the incursion of Japan onto the mainland, with the invasion of Manchukuo) caused diversion of resources towards rearmament and the building-up of war industries. For example, the Second Five Year Plan initially provided for some relaxation, with rather more emphasis upon consumers' goods, only to be revised upwards again in the course of the quinquennium because of increasing tension in the international situation. In face of a sharply adverse movement in the terms of foreign trade in 1930 (due to the world economic crisis and the sharp price-fall of agricultural products on world markets) and a succession of bad harvests in the early '30s, coupled with a sharp decline of livestock in the wake of the collectivisation 'drive', it is scarcely surprising that acute shortages should have developed, alike of foodstuffs for the swollen urban population and of an increasing range of building and constructional materials and other industrial supplies. Just as rationing of scarce foodstuffs had to be introduced for consumers between 1931 and 1934, so it became the practice, as shortages of industrial supplies became acute, for these to be rationed between industries, and between enterprises within an industry, by a system of centrally-determined allocations, as had happened in the years preceding NEP. When shortcomings in plan-fulfilment occurred – when, for example, certain items in an 'assortment' of products were neglected in favour of others, or output-targets were fulfilled to the neglect of cost-reduction or even at the expense of inflated costs or a swollen employment-figure – the tendency was to meet this in subsequent years by adding to the plan express stipulations about 'product-assortment' or about cost-reduction and labour-employment. As a supplementary instrument of control, especially over wage-expenditures and the holding of stocks by industrial enterprises, there was developed an increasingly detailed Credit-Plan, stipulating the amount of credit that Banks were allowed to grant to industry for specific purposes. This was closely related to the Production-plan of the enterprise in question, and included strictly limited provision for supplementary or 'above plan' credits to meet exceptional situations or needs.

The leading planning method that was developed during this period was the so-called 'method of material balances'. A 'balance' consisted of an equation between the available supplies and the demands upon a particular product; and it constituted the indispensable instrument in deciding upon the needed 'funded supplies' for the purpose of the allocation system and also for gearing together the constituent elements of the total production plan. Crucial to these balances were the so-called 'technical coefficients', expressing the input-output relationship of various products. These coefficients, however, would be different for different production-plants engaged on the same product according to their technical equipment and general efficiency; moreover, it was very often official policy to raise and tighten those above what the industries themselves might feel to be 'objectively possible' or what past experience had shown to be the prevailing relationship. Information coming to the centre from lower levels about the supply of inputs needed to fulfil a certain output programme was not necessarily unbiased (since industrial managers would find life easier for themselves and their employees and be better able to meet their plan-targets and handle unforeseen eventualities if they had something in reserve); and if planners suspected such bias they tended to offset it by correspondingly 'tightening' the coefficients. For any particular industry the appropriate coefficient was a weighted average dependent on the particular make-up of its production-plan, and hence was subject to change if this plan was altered either in the final stages of plan revision or in course of its implementation; and they contained inevitably a certain 'subjective' or policy-element. A further problem was that of coordinating individual balances to allow for criss-cross dependencies or so-called 'feedback' relationships (a problem familiar to input-output analysts in terms of the 'inversion of a matrix'). Soviet planners at this period paid little attention to developing more refined 'balance methodology' such as was to be developed in the West in the form of Leontief's input-output analysis. Perhaps it would have made little difference to actual practice if they had (at any rate without the extensive aid of electronic computers); since the requirements of the planning time-table impose fairly strict limits upon the number of stages or 'linkage-effects' that can be calculated when any given production-target is revised (it has been the customary practice, indeed, to extend the calculation to no more than what are termed 'second order' or 'third order' linkages at most).

For all these reasons no more than *approximate* consistency, or 'internal fit', could be provided for in the best-constructed operative plan. The supply-allocation system was almost bound to involve shortages for some industries and industrial enterprises, even if those crucial input-output coefficients had been realistically assessed. What can be said, however, is that any resulting maladjustments were not likely to result in cumulative fluctuations characteristic of a market-system (*vide* the economists' 'cobweb-type' fluctuation) and that the resulting coordination, although imperfect, is likely to be greater than with atomistic decisions about output and investment taken in face of uncertainty of each decision-taker about the future shape and trend of the total situation.

With rapid growth, characterised by large structural change, as the prime objective of economic policy at this period, it was not at all unnatural that planning should have the character of 'priority planning', in the sense that it was influenced by, and operated in terms of, a priority-list of objectives. The order of priorities might change over time as the nature of the particular 'bottlenecks' obstructing advance altered. But throughout this pre-war period one priority continued to dominate: so-called 'priority for heavy industry' – expansion of the capital goods sector of industry, basic fuel and power and metals and machine-making. To this was joined, as we have seen, priority for 'defence industry' and developments auxiliary thereto – an objective that steadily increased in weight as the Second Five Year Plan followed on the heels of the First and after it the (unfinished) Third, which was dominated by the three priority objectives of war industry, non-ferrous metals and transport-extension. Indeed, by the end of the decade the economy of the country could be said to have virtually constituted a war economy, with the methods and degree of centralisation customary thereto.

In one respect this priority-element in planning policy made the problems of a highly centralised system of planning and economic administration much easier – although not without an attendant social cost. The objectives and targets of the high-priority sectors were more easy to fulfil, because, if anything went wrong, resources could be transferred to them from the low-priority sectors. Thus the latter played the role of a cushion or reserve for any deficiency in plan fulfilment on the part of the former. These low-priority industries (which in those days were usually the consumers' goods industries) bore the brunt of the situation, in that they failed to fulfil their own plan-targets; but the essential priorities were safeguarded and were generally able to be fulfilled (at anyrate in the broad and the round). But in the degree to which quantitative growth and heavy industry lost their priority, and this shifted to the consumers' goods industries (as it began to do in the '50s) the situation changed. Either priority could be regarded as being more widely distributed, or the need for 'balance' between a variety of competing needs as replacing the practice of working down a simply-ordered priority-list. In either case the situation and its associated problems changed, and the easy 'reserve' that low-priority sectors had previously constituted ceased to exist.

This was one respect in which the situation changed between the pre-war decade and the period of the '50s, following the end of post-war reconstruction. But there were others as well. One of these was the situation in the labour market affecting the overall labour supply. The initial ten or twelve years of planning had been a period of 'extensive growth' in the sense of a 'widening' of the scope and range of existing industry (together with the foundation of new ones such as motors and aircraft and non-ferrous metals) by drawing upon reserves of labour in the countryside. When the targets for higher labour productivity in the First Five Year Plan failed to be fulfilled, this failure could be compensated for by an above-plan expansion in employment (although this had inflationary consequences from enlarging the total wage-bill and hence demand). It is true, of course, that there were shortages of skilled labour even at this period – shortages that were met by large-scale training schemes. But in general there was no shortage of unskilled labour, since in common with most other backward areas of the world Russian agriculture had been characterised (save in areas of fairly recent settlement like Siberia and the Far East) by rural over-population. By 1950, following upon enormous war-losses, the situation with regard to labour supply was beginning to change. 'Extensive' growth was beginning to meet limits in general, not only, in particular, labour shortage. Increased emphasis came to be placed upon higher labour productivity by means of technical innovation and modernisation. Once again achievement failed to match intention; and much of the trouble with slackened growth-rates in the early '60s was no doubt attributable to a 'lag' in 'intensive' development of the kind which the new and changed situation required.

In addition to changes in the nature of policy-objectives which planning was required to serve and changes in the labour-situation, the very growth of industry in the pre-war period made the tasks of centralised planning much more complex, and hence considerably augmented those difficulties of the balance-method that we have already mentioned and the negative effects of resulting failures and inconsistencies in the provisions of the plan (especially in connection with the allocation system for 'funded' supplies). Whereas at the start of the '30s the number of separate balances handled by Gosplan did not exceed a few hundred, by the decade of the '50s this figure had grown to nearly 2000 (including in this figure those handled by both the Republican Gosplans and the all-Union Gosplan). Something like 10,000 products or more were covered by the system of central supply-allocations (so-called 'funded commodities') and more than 5000 products, with their appropriate targets and 'indices', had come to be listed in the annual plan (and in the plan for a single enterprise there could be as many as 500 separate indices). By the '60s the number of separate industrial enterprises to be planned for reached the figure of 40,000.

DISCUSSION OF TRENDS TOWARD DECENTRALISATION

It was against this background that the discussions of the late '50s and '60s started about the need for measures of decentralisation.

Highly centralised methods, appropriate as they may well have been to the situation and to the special policy-objectives and tasks of the pre-war decade, as also of the 'war economy' of the '40s, were evidently becoming increasingly inappropriate to the changed situation of the '50s, and were even showing negative results upon which critical comment was beginning to concentrate. Such discussion was not confined to the Soviet Union, but extended to the other countries of the socialist *bloc* in Eastern Europe; being most intense, and going furthest in the decentralising measures advocated, in Czechoslovakia and Hungary, and being relatively muted in the DDR (East Germany) and Roumania, with Poland and also Bulgaria falling somewhere in between. In this atmosphere were prepared and implemented the economic reforms of the middle '60s (sometimes being called, as in Hungary, the introduction of 'the new economic model'). There was general recognition of the need to simplify the tasks of central planning by reducing the number of targets and indices fixed by the topmost bodies and included in the central plan, and at the same time by giving greater autonomy and discretion to the individual enterprises, in the interest of encouraging a greater measure of initiative (e.g. as regards innovation both in methods of production and in types of output, new products and models etc.) on the part of managements at the enterprise or plant level. Where emphasis differed, and the precise character of the decentralising measures, was (1) as to whether the actual enterprises or new intermediate-level industrial associations (operating on the basis of *Khozraschot*) were to be the main beneficiaries of increased latitude and autonomy, (2) as to how far greater flexibility was introduced as regards prices and procurement of industrial supplies on a contractual basis – in other words, how far some measure of market-mechanism was re-introduced into inter-industrial exchange, reminiscent of the period of the Soviet NEP in the 1920s. In Hungary, for example, the supply allocation system was terminated, and the prices of a fairly large category of goods were allowed to vary contractually within upper and lower price-limits, while in the case of a minority of things (largely luxuries) prices could vary without limit according to the state of the market. Even some investment expenditures (below a certain size) could be undertaken at the discretion of enterprises, with the aid of bank-loans.

In terms of the economists' debate of the inter-war period, this might seem to be a reversion to the kind of decentralised mechanism, or 'market socialism' as this has sometimes been called, that was outlined by Dickinson and Lange. This, however, is no more than partially true. In the Dickinson and Lange proposals there was very little room left for planning. Almost all economic decision was taken on the basis of, and was governed by, the market: in Lange's case with the exception only of the general rate of investment, or the *total* investment fund to be placed at the disposal of economic bodies (its *allocation* among industries being decided by demand in relation to the given supply). But in the decentralised mechanism introduced by the economic reforms in the '60s, there remained considerably more scope for central planning than this. In the main, even in Hungary, investment remained predominantly under central control; and although enterprises were free to construct their own annual output plans, these were supposed to be geared fairly closely to a longer-term plan drawn up by the central planning bodies; while the prices of all 'key' products (and certainly of scarce commodities) were still fixed by central control. There was no such dismantling of planning here as occurred in Yugoslavia in the '50s. In the case of the Soviet reform of 1965, while the indices in the annual plan were much reduced in number, certain crucial ones remained so far as an enterprise was concerned: in particular, total *marketed* output in value terms (this replacing gross value produced as previously) and a 'limit' on its total wage-bill. Balance-sheet profit was recognised as the main criterion of enterprise-performance (and a new type of incentive-fund, with attached bonuses, geared thereto); but the allocation system with regard to supplies continued in existence.

The first criticism to be heard of the previous over-centralised system related to the way in which plan-targets had necessarily to be expressed in plan-directives – criticism that applied especially to those that were in terms of some physical dimension. Obviously if output at the enterprise level is controlled in detail by the plan, it must be expressed in some dimension or other; and experience has shown that the particular dimension chosen may have a distorting effect on the way in which the plan-target is achieved. In some cases the most appropriate measure of output is in terms of weight – in others of length or surface-area or simple number of items. There are by now numerous and well-known examples where measurement in terms of weight creates a bias in favour of producing heavy objects rather than light (as with bedsteads or chandeliers or nails), or where it is in terms of length, as with cloth, a bias in favour of narrow cloth of simplest-possible weave; and so forth. Where output is heterogeneous rather than uniform and standardised, as is the case with a lot of engineering products, the most easy measure is in terms of gross value (which has the advantage of simplicity in that items can be added-up at their current selling-price). But experience has, again, shown that, in the case of gross value, distortion takes the form of encouraging an inflation of the amount of inputs (purchased from outside the enterprise) that are embodied in the product: use, for example, of expensive rather than cheap materials and components – the production of so-called 'material-intensive' types of product. Another example is that it will prove more easy to fulfil a plan-target by assembling a large mass of components into a finished vehicle, rather than by supplying separately specialised spare parts even when the latter are in great demand. It may also discourage the vertical integration of successive processes under the same enterprise, even where this would result in greater efficiency and a more balanced and coordinated production-flow (although, this influence may be counterbalanced by supply-difficulties and delays which encourage the tendency to vertical integration); for this reason, in the late '50s and early '60s gross value was abandoned in favour of net value in a large number of industries, beginning with the clothing industry.

Whatever the precise form that measurement takes, targets of this kind inevitably tend to give a premium to purely quantitative fulfilment, to the neglect of qualitative considerations, of the requirements of a balanced assortment, and above all of the search for new products and new and improved designs. It likewise tends to put a premium on quantitative fulfilment even at the expense of inefficiencies: *vide* the common habit of 'storming', or excessive speed-up and overtime, towards the end of a plan-period. It was to counteract such effects, indeed, that the so-called 'qualitative indices' were added to the plan-directives, stipulating such things as the degree of cost-reduction to be achieved or the amount of increase of labour productivity. But this had the effect of inflating the number and variety of types of 'indices' written into the plan-indices to which different weight came to be attached by enterprise managements, some standing in conflict with others and some tending accordingly to be ignored altogether.

It was consideration of the disadvantages and distortions arising from the various types of 'success indicators' previously in use as an almost inevitable accompaniment of including excessive detail in the central plan, that attention was turned to the need for some 'synthetic index' of enterprise achievement, which would serve at anyrate to minimise the one-sided distorting effects of existing indices. (A common slogan of the time was 'less reliance on administrative directives and more reliance on economic methods', e.g. price-inducements, credit facilities, taxes and the like.) To this end the economic reforms of the middle '60s not unnaturally tended to give more weight to balance-sheet results, as a measure of achievement, as in early years of *Khozraschot*, in the degree to which reliance on the method of detailed directives was reduced. But, of course, 'balance-sheet' criteria can also have 'distorting' effects upon output if prices are not 'right' in some appropriate sense – a reason why measures of price-reform accompanied measures of decentralisation (and in the Hungarian case preceded the introduction of the 'new economic mechanism').

Another type of criticism of the older centralised system was its tendency to generate damaging forms of tension between upper and lower levels in the degree to which it narrowed the competence of the latter (and this about matters on which the latter very often knew best). To some extent, of course, this could be represented as a clash between sectional viewpoints or interests and the general interest. Yet this was by no means always so. It was almost if not quite as much a conflict between decisions on detail taken by persons remote from the actual situation (on the basis of imperfect and very approximate information) and detailed knowledge of that situation by those close to it and possessed not only of technical information but also of a 'feel' for what could be done. Two principal examples of this were as follows. First, under constant pressure (coupled with financial inducement) to fulfil (probably over-tight) plan-targets, and haunted by the constant fear of supply shortages and delivery-delays, seriously disruptive of production, industrial managements would tend, in the information they supplied to higher levels, to understate and conceal productive possibilities and overstate their needs (as regards supplies, equipment, labour). We have already said that, if the planning bodies or Ministries suspected such a bias, they would react to it by tightening output-targets and reducing allocations, thus cumulatively enhancing the polar tension between 'levels'. (It was a common saying at the time that a wise director may overfulfil his plan by, say, 5 per cent, but never by 25 per cent – if he did, the result would inevitably be that his target for the ensuing year would be drastically revised upward). Secondly, strong encouragement was given, not only to overstating supply-requirements, in order to give 'elbow-room for manoeuvre' (i.e. restore some flexibility at the enterprise level) and provide for unforeseen contingencies, but whenever possible accumulating excessive reserves, whether of equipment, materials or labour. This was the sole remaining way in which enterprise managements could restore initiative to themselves. It is well-known that hoarding tends to aggravate supply-shortages and probably cumulatively so. This may well have had a good deal to do with accentuating and perpetuating in the post-war period the chronic situation of 'sellers' market', which was in turn used by conservative centralisers as a reason for continued rationing by means of the system of supply-allocations.

Marxists in particular may feel, further, that with a chain of command excessively pendant on orders from the top, with those below inured to passive reception of orders and directives, the 'alienation' of the rank-and-file producer from the social process as a whole may be perpetuated rather than overcome.

Hitherto the movement towards economic reform of a decentralising kind has so far been cautious and fairly limited (except in Hungary and Yugoslavia) – and more limited in implementation than in design, if only because of the hesitancy and resistance of bureaucratic interests associated with the previous system. But the future trend seems likely to be in this direction. Experience appears to show the difficulties and negative effects of too great centralisation of decision-taking. It remains for experiment and comparative experience to demonstrate what *degree* of blend of planning and market will yield, in normal circumstances, the superior result: what category of decision deserves to remain centralised, and embodied in an obligatory plan, what is better left for decision, at subordinate levels, on the basis of market-indices (prices whether actual or 'accounting'), in the manner proposed by Dickinson and Lange in the pre-war economists' debate; with planning confined in their case to influencing (e.g. by taxes, credit-availabilities, price-changes) and general 'steering'. It looks fairly clear that decisions regarding major new investment, crucial as these are to the long-term trend of the economy, to structural shifts, to the employment-level and to growth, are likely to fall into the former (the centralised) category; and there seem to be fairly strong theoretical grounds for their doing so.

THE PROBLEM OF PRICES

But once market influences upon economic decision-taking are reintroduced into the picture, then of course the question of what are 'correct' or 'economic' prices, as we have said, assumes importance; and here we are back at some stage of the economic theorists' discussion, especially the later discussions about price-policy and so-called 'optimising'. Even in centralised planning some calculations involve prices, although these need not be actual prices in the sense of ratios at which things exchange: they may be no more than calculation-prices in the sense of Lange's 'ratios of equivalence' (*vide* ratios such as the 'recoupment period' or 'effectiveness of investment'). In connection with linear programming solutions, the idea of 'shadow prices' as the 'dual' of any given solution is nowadays sufficiently familiar. Discussion of such questions has characterised the Soviet economic scene since the middle '50s as well as elsewhere. Discussion about the so-called 'operation of the law of value' started in the middle '50s in a rather abstract and doctrinaire fashion. But this very soon developed into a contest between rival advocates of 'the value principle' and of 'prices of production', which was intended to have a concrete reference to the reform of price-policy; and in the course of this the mathematical economists' advocacy of so-called 'Kantorovitch *otsenki*' assumed an increasing prominence in the debate. The Price Reform of 1968 represented in many respects a compromise between rival viewpoints, and in a number of respects an interim one; but it bore the clear impress of the preceding discussion, and it paid tribute at least in principle to such notions as an equal profit-rate, rental charges for use of natural resources or to take account of advantages of situation.

In the West discussion among economists (to a large extent a sequel to the debate about socialist calculation in the '30s) was preoccupied mainly with two kinds of issue: treatment of cases (e.g. where there were substantial indivisibilities) where marginal cost diverged from average cost, and treatment of the 'peak' and 'off-peak' problem, where, as in cases like electricity or transport, over-capacity use and under-capacity use of equipment alternated at different times of the day or week or at different seasons. Initially the advocates of marginal cost pricing used this as a critical weapon for attacking accepted doctrine to the effect that nationalised industries must be made to 'pay' (i.e. cover average total cost including some conventional rate of profit). Hence the emphasis on cases where average costs were falling with expansion of output or of service-supplied, and hence marginal cost was below average cost. These were essentially cases of excess capacity existing within an indivisible unit; and the commonsense argument was that there was social advantage in making use of excess capacity so long as the prime or direct costs involved in this additional use was covered, and that there would be social waste of resources if additional use of spare capacity were precluded by an attempt to charge a price equal to the full (average) cost (as private capitalist enterprise would of course, do). Another aspect of the same argument was the contention that in the case in question the proper investment criterion was that of 'total social benefit' (*not* the criterion of covering total cost at a uniform price) – as illustrated by the classic case of Dupuit's bridge.

But while such cases where marginal cost was less than average cost existed and were undoubtedly important (some would claim that they preponderated among cases of divergence) they did not stand alone. There were also rising-cost cases where marginal cost stood above and not below average; and as regards practice these were apt to involve greater difficulty. Where they were not simply cases of social costs external to the decision-unit in question, as in the traffic-congestion case, they were apt to be examples of alternating over-capacity and under-capacity use of fixed equipment at different times, as with electricity-generation, a telephone network or a railway transport system. Here the case for differential charging between peak and off-peak usage (related to the difference in marginal cost of supplying service at times of under-utilised capacity and over-use of capacity) was based essentially on avoidance of wasteful investment in expanding capacity to adapt it to peak-demand –wasteful because this would involve excessive unused capacity at other times.

When we come to discussion of a general pricing-principle for regulating pricing in a socialist economy, we are confronted with an apparent conflict of objectives. This may be described as one between short-period and long-period (or alternatively between so-called 'market prices' and 'normal prices'). At any given moment of time there is likely to be a given 'pattern' of scarcities, containing what may be called 'accidental' elements, due to unforeseen demand-shifts, or shifts in stocks or adjustment time-lags in supply. Complete equilibrium at that moment would impose a certain pattern of short-period prices adjusted to this given pattern of scarcities – prices which from their nature may be no more than temporary and may well not persist into subsequent periods, after there has been time for supply-adjustments to occur. This will at anyrate be the case unless stocks are capable of taking the brunt of short-period disequilibrium, which they may well be able to do to a greater extent than is sometimes allowed for, at least for quite short periods if the demand-shifts are sufficiently moderate. In the one case the price-movement, in the other case the movement of stocks, can serve as 'indicators' to producers of requisite adjustments of supply. As we have seen, however, too great reliance on, or latitude for, such short-period adjustments may give scope to undesirably disorganising cumulative fluctuations of the 'cobweb theorem' type.

When one comes, however, to consider what may be called 'long-period decisions' such as investment in durable equipment (e.g. a new plant, railway line, dock or electrical power plant) a different kind of price is relevant – what may be called a 'long-term normal price', in the sense of one that would represent an equilibrium-adaptation over a period of years long enough for supply-adaptations to be fully made to whatever was the probable level of demand in those future years. This is some kind of cost price (and according to a theorem, now well-known to economists, a cost-price that includes a profit-rate, if growth is occurring, and one approximately equal to that growth-rate).

If prices were all 'accounting prices' of the Lange-type or else 'calculation prices' or shadow-prices, used in a central planning-office for purpose of estimating as a basis of decisions, the conflict would be apparent rather than real. Whichever category of price, whether short-period or long-period, was appropriate to the particular decision that was involved could be used in that calculation, and this would not preclude the use of a different and contrasted category in other decisions of a different type. But where the prices are actual prices, representing actual exchange-ratios at which things change hands between financially autonomous bodies (on a *Khozraschot* basis) and in terms of which contracts are made, the conflict is a real one, since in actual fact the prices in question must be of one kind or another, and there could scarcely be two different sets of prices existing simultaneously (although there could presumably be 'spot' and 'future' prices for transactions at different dates). Evidently the category of short-period price is the appropriate one for the retail market, if rationing is to be avoided and also shop-shortages and queues in the case of scarce commodity-lines. Perhaps it is appropriate too to the factory selling-price of consumers' goods (although it is quite possible to have these based on some other principle and the difference between them and the retail price to be bridged by some kind of turnover tax as has been the Soviet practice). But what of the pricing of so-called producers' goods – things which serve as inputs to production, and especially constructional materials and machine-tools? These are the components or objects of investment decisions and of decisions involving choice of technique or of input-combinations, and seem to be more suitable objects for the other category of price. Of course, certain items of this type may be associated with problems of temporary scarcity, requiring that this should be recognised by a (temporarily imposed) mark-up on the 'normal' price as a way both of enforcing economy in their use and of confining them to the most urgent uses so long as this scarcity lasts. But departures from 'normal' cost could probably here be treated as exceptional rather than (as in the retail market) as the general rule.

CONCLUSION

In summary one can say that the most conspicuous achievements of planning are connected with economic growth and with large-scale structural changes in the economic system, involving a changing relationship between economic sectors and industries, possibly also changes in industrial location and the pattern of transport networks appropriate thereto. *A fortiori* to this are social objectives and inter-relationships (e.g. environmental factors, employment effects, creation of wants or of attitudes, 'ways of life' and social standards) such as would fail to secure recognition in purely market and balance-sheet terms. Despite the industrialising achievements of capitalist enterprise under *laissez-faire* conditions in the past, it is quite possible that, in the absence of planning, certain types of development may fail to take place at all because of the structural interdependencies involved (development at one point being unprofitable unless it is known that appropriate complementary developments will take place at a number of other points), and/or because against certain types of obstacle the momentum of development, once started, is difficult to maintain and hence growth peters out. For these reasons planning in one form or another has become in recent decades a part of the creed of an increasingly wide circle of underdeveloped countries.

Since most if not all countries of the present-day world are growing economies in varying degree, one cannot in practice separate problems of growth and those of balanced adjustment to a given level of consumption-demand (or problems of 'optimising' as economists have come to call it). But in so far as the latter takes precedence over the former, then we have seen that there emerges an advantage in decentralising a considerable degree, at least, of detailed decision-taking, and hence of combining market mechanism and influence with the larger framework of centrally steered or planned macro-decision. In such circumstances, and with regard to this type of objective, overcentralisation, by reducing flexibility and congesting the apparatus of decision-taking, may actually hamper adjustment and preclude 'optimising' both as regards adaptation of production to consumers' wants and as regards efficient choice of methods of production and of allocation.

Thus the focus of earlier theoretical debate about planning has been significantly shifted, and in an important sense has become less simple. Few if any economists who discuss such matters today are prepared to accept the simple *non possumus* of von Mises, if only for the reason that few of them, either in the capitalist or the socialist world, accept 'planning' and 'market' as mutually-exclusive antitheses. Discussion has shifted rather to the question of what is the most appropriate and practicable blend of the two –

a question which again may well permit of different answers in different sets of historical circumstances, with their different levels of development. It cannot be denied that the above-cited problem of the 'millions of equations' requiring to be solved if decisions are to be made and coordinated consciously has been powerfully affected, even if it has not been completely solved, by the invention and use of electronic computers. And here, perhaps, one should allow Oskar Lange to have the last word. In what was probably his last utterance on the matter, Professor Lange wrote about 'Planning and the Computer' as follows (in partial redressing of the balance of his earlier decentralising proposals): 'Managers of socialist economies to-day have two instruments of economic accounting. One is the electronic computer ... the other is the market ... Experience shows that for a very large number of problems linear approximation suffices; hence the widespread use of linear programming techniques ... The computer has the undoubted advantage of much greater speed. The market is a cumbersome and slow-working servo-mechanism. Its iteration process operates with considerable time-lags and oscillations and may not be convergent at all'. After stating, however, that 'even the most powerful electronic computer has a limited capacity', he concludes that for planning long-term economic development the market mechanism is definitely inferior ('actual market equilibrium prices do not suffice here, knowledge of the programmed future shadow prices is needed'). 'Mathematical programming', he declares, 'turns out to be an essential instrument of *optimal* long-term economic planning ... Mathematical programming assisted by electronic computers becomes the fundamental instrument of long-term economic planning, as well as of solving dynamic economic problems of a more limited scope. Here, the electronic computer does not replace the market. It fulfils a function which the market never was able to perform' (in C.H. Feinstein (edited), *Socialism, Capitalism and Economic Growth*, Cambridge 1967, pp158-61).

BIBLIOGRAPHY

Ch. Bettelheim, *Problèmes Thèoriques et Pratiques de la Planification*, Paris 1946, 2nd ed. 1951.

Mikhail Bor, *Aims and Methods of Soviet Planning*, London 1967.

G.D.H. Cole, *Principles of Economic Planning*, London 1935.

M.H. Dobb, *An Essay on Economic Growth and Planning*, London 1960.

M.H. Dobb, *Soviet Economic Development since 1917* (revised sixth edition), London 1966, esp. Chapters 10, 14, 15.

M.H. Dobb, *Welfare Economics and the Economics of Socialism*, Cambridge 1967, esp. Chapters 7, 8, 9.

H.D. Dickinson, 'Price Formation in a Socialist Community', in *The Economic Journal*, June 1933.

H.D. Dickinson, *The Economics of Socialism*, Oxford 1939.

Michael Ellman, *Soviet Planning Today*, Cambridge 1971.

C.H. Feinstein (ed), *Socialism, Capitalism and Economic Growth*, Cambridge 1967.

G. Grossman (ed), *Essays in Socialism and Planning in Honor of Carl Landauer*, New Jersey 1970.

R.L. Hall, *The Economic System in a Socialist State*, London 1937.

F. von Hayek (ed.), *Collectivist Economic Planning*, London 1935.

Branko Horvat, *Towards a Theory of Planned Economy*, Beograd 1964.

János Kornai, *Overcentralization in Economic Administration*, Oxford 1959.

Carl Landauer, *Theory of National Economic Planning*, Los Angeles 1947.

Carl Landauer, *Planwirtschaft und Verkehrswirtschaft*, Munich-Leipzig 1931.

Carl Landauer, *European Socialism*, 2 vols., Berkeley (USA) 1959.

Oskar Lange, *On the Economic Theory of Socialism*, Minnesota (USA) 1938.

F. von Mises, *Socialism* (trans. J. Kahane), London 1936.

Alec Nove, *The Soviet Economy*, London 1961.

A.C. Pigou, *Socialism versus Capitalism*, London 1937.

Ota Šik, *Plan and Market under Socialism*, Prague 1967.

Benjamin Ward, *The Socialist Economy: a Study of Organizational Alternatives*, New York 1967.

J. Wilczynski, *The Economics of Socialism*, London 1970.

Barbara Wootton, *Plan or No Plan*, London 1934.

Commodity-production under socialism

NEP as a period in the development of the Soviet economy has receded sufficiently into past history, eclipsed as the '20s have been by so many subsequent issues and dramatic developments, as to have apparently lost all interest, even significance, for the discussion of socialism and its problems. It was, after all, half a century ago; and many have regarded it, then and since, as a temporary aberration on the road to socialism, cradled in certain special and largely transitory problems. Now that the issue of centralisation *versus* decentralisation has come upon the agenda of socialist debate (and not only in the sphere of economic administration and functioning) may there not be something to be said for taking a new and backward look at NEP and at some of the contemporary assessments of it – and this is *not* just for reasons of historical curiosity?

Some stimulus in this direction has indeed been given by the publication of a recent Hungarian work by Laszlo Szamuely (it appeared in English translation in 1974) – an enlarged essay rather than a comprehensive study, and evidently a product of thinking and debate around the so-called 'new economic mechanism' in Hungary.[1] To my mind it has the virtue of being unusually outspoken. Szamuely at the end of his three-page Introduction sounds the keynote of this reassessment as he regards it by saying:

> The raising of these questions may seem mere hairsplitting, yet the clarification of a problem of much broader relevance depends on the answer; namely, which of the functional models of socialist economy was theoretically and practically the initial pattern of the socialist socio-economic system: a centralised subsistence economy, managed by instructions, based on equalitarian princi-

> ples, or a regulated market economy, relying on material incentives? If this problem can be sufficiently clarified, the substance of NEP will also appear in a different light.

and not merely as:

> a 'historical' issue, since half a century of socialist economic development could not reduce the significance of this problem to one relevant only to the past.

Putting it more bluntly, the issue boils down to the question whether and why the 'first stage of socialism' (in Marx's sense, or 'socialist' contrasted with 'communism' – something that evidently is destined to occupy a whole historical period and is *not* just transition) is compatible or incompatible with the existence of commodity-production, or market-relations? It is clear that many of the extreme Left today, and particularly Maoists (an example familiar to some of us is Bettelheim), believe that anything deserving the name of socialism is incompatible with commodity-production. (Mandel also speaks of commodity production dying out under socialism, but in the degree to which a 'social wage' replaces a *money* wage – and be it noted he makes no distinction between the lower and the higher stage of socialism.) Szamuely claims (and cites evidence in support) that this was the traditional view held not only by 19th century social democrats like Kautsky, but also by Bukharin and Lenin (at one time at least). Developed socialism was envisaged as being essentially a '*natural* economy' (by contrast with a monetary or exchange economy). With reference to German Social-Democracy Szamuely says: 'the view that socialist economy excludes market relations and realises a "natural" economy ha(d) become a dogma. In various refined forms, this dogma ruled in Marxist political economy for over half a century and caused extremely great damage to the development of socialist economy' (p.24).

Historically the matter is usually considered to start with 'War Communism' (which is the subject of Szamuely's first chapter). Some might say it really opens with the first eight months of the Soviet revolution prior to the onset of Civil war and Foreign intervention since economic relations then closely resembled those of NEP. Before proceeding with this perhaps I should insert in parenthesis the confession that I really have nothing new to say about all this, going beyond restatement of what has been said before by myself at times and by others. Please do not expect more than a recapitulation of arguments and issues.

WAR COMMUNISM

'War Communism', which developed rapidly after the summer of 1918, had the following distinctive features, as you may remember (in addition to the extension of state ownership to quite small enterprises employing more than five workers). Firstly, both work-discipline and allocation of labour as between jobs and places. By the end of the civil war, indeed, there were a lot of explicit reference to 'militarisation of labour' (one sometimes wonders how many romantic leftists have seriously faced up to the fact that if one is not to have material incentives to work, one must have compulsion to labour in some form, at least in the last resort?). Secondly, direct central allocation of supplies (i.e. raw materials and components and equipment) to industry, as well as centralised direction (by orders from above) of all productive activity. Thirdly, the direct allocation of consumers' goods between individuals and/or families by a system of rationing (not always egalitarian but socially graded as between categories). Fourthly, and in Russia's situation quite crucially, the compulsory seizure or requisitioning of the surplus of agricultural supplies from peasant producers. By the end of the period there was even talk of compulsory sowing plans (adopted in principle at the 8th Congress of Soviets) because compulsory requisitioning was exerting a catastrophically adverse effect on the sown area.

As war-time improvisation in face of acute economic difficulties and shortages (approaching famine conditions in the end), this is all comprehensible enough, and scarcely needs detailed explanation. But what is significant in our present context is that it was at the time explicitly justified, *not* by temporary necessity, but as the dawning of true socialism or communism – and this evidently *not* just as a propaganda exercise to put a gloss on the face of war-time scarcity. While Preobrazhensky's much-quoted reference to the inflationary printing-presses of the period as a 'machine-gun attacking the bourgeois *regime* in the rear, namely through its monetary system' could possibly be treated as a propaganda flourish, the same could not be said of the solemn declaration in an official journal in 1920 of the head of the State Bank and later chairman of the Supreme Council of National Economy Obolensky-Ossinsky that 'our financial policy has been aimed recently at building up a financial system based on the emission of paper money, the ultimate objective of which is the natural transition to distribution of goods without using money'. Indeed, the Programme of the Bolshevik Party adopted in 1919 spoke of the introduction of 'several measures to expand the scope of cashless transactions, and to prepare for the abolition of money'. Bukharin in his *Economics of the Transition Period* written at this time sponsors the idea of a natural and rapid transition to a system of moneyless social accounting, with 'extra-economic coercion' during the period of transition playing a positive organisational and disciplinary role. Larin and Piatakov also sponsored this view, as did L. Kritsman, historian of 'war communism', who as late as 1924 writing under the title of *The Heroic Period of the Great Russian Revolution*, spoke of this 'first grandiose attempt at proletarian natural economy [and] to make the first steps of transition to socialism' as being 'the *anticipation of the future*, the breaking of the future into the present (which is now past).'

Be it noted also that it was not until 12 months after what was thought to be the end of the war (i.e. after the defeat of Kolchak and Denikin) that 'War Communism' was terminated by Lenin's famous intervention. During these twelve months there was talk of extending and completing the regimentation characteristic of 'War Communism' and not reducing it (such as the compulsory sowings we have mentioned); and discussion was about such things as the role of trade unions and Trotsky's proposed 'labour army' to be concentrated successively on key economic fronts (called by some the 'stateisation' of TUs). It was the disastrous harvest results of the winter of '20-'21, combined with the Tambov rising and the Kronstadt revolt, that prompted Lenin's sharp turn to the NEP in the spring of 1921.

NEW ECONOMIC POLICY

But – and this was a pretty big 'but' – the circumstances in which the NEP was introduced made it almost inevitable that emphasis should be placed on the position of the peasantry – on the necessity of restoring the alliance between working class and peasantry (the *smytchka*). While dismissing War Communism as a 'temporary policy' and not 'a policy that corresponded to the economic tasks of the proletariat' – even a 'mistake' and a 'jump' that stood 'in complete contradiction to all we wrote concerning the transition from capitalism to socialism' – Lenin started from the substitution of free trading in grain (combined with an agricultural tax, first in kind and then in money) for compulsory requisitioning, from which other measures of a more general kind later followed. The consequence was that the 'retreat' to NEP, as Lenin on at least one occasion called it, was attributed to the distance of an individualist, unsocialised and at the time unsocialisable peasantry – primarily if not solely to this. This remained more or less, the official view (if adapted somewhat to cover the era of collectivisation) up to the time of Stalin's last work, *Economic Problems of Socialism in the USSR* (1952), where the continuance of commodity production (and hence 'the law of value') is explicitly attributed to the existence of two forms (or sectors) of socialist property (fully socialised industry and the cooperative or collective farms) – although it is true that a subordinate place is given to 'the exchange of articles of personal consumption' needed 'to compensate the labour power expended in the process of production' and 'realised as commodities'. It is stated here quite categorically, however, that when 'instead of the two basic production sectors, the state sector and the collective farm sector, there will be only one all-embracing production sector ... commodity circulation, with its "money-economy", will disappear, as being an unnecessary element in the national economy'.

As for the official *Political Economy* textbook of the mid-50s (1954), this speaks of NEP (the principles of which, it said, had been 'worked out by Lenin in the spring of 1918') as an economic policy in the transitional period 'for building socialism while utilising the market, trade and monetary circulation', and likewise found 'the essence of this policy' in 'an economic alliance of the working class and the peasantry, which was necessary in order to draw the peasant masses into socialist construction'. As regards War Communism, this was 'inevitable in the given historical conditions, those of civil war and economic breakdown'. But it was 'incompatible with the bond between town and country', and a proletarian State 'can therefore avoid War Communism in the absence of intervention and economic ruin resulting from a prolonged war', as witness the People's Democracies. The Kuusinen book of the late '50s (*Fundamentals of Marxism-Leninism*, Eng. ed. 1961) had this to say:

> At this stage of development of productive forces and social property characteristic of socialism, the main economic operations, such as planned distribution of labour among different branches of the national economy and distribution of the means of production and consumer goods, cannot take place without utilising commodity-money relations or forms of value. This in no way contradicts the principles of socialism.

Despite this statement one is left with the implication that commodity-forms will disappear at a more mature stage of socialism. It then goes on to repeat what Stalin said about the two forms of socialist property, while adding one or two other reasons as well: 'the great advantage of commodity production' (it says) 'retains its importance so long as there is a distinction between the labour of the worker and of the collective farmer, between skilled and unskilled labour, between mental and physical labour, and as long as society cannot simply measure the labour expended in the manufacture of a given commodity in hours of labour time' (p.710). It also goes beyond Stalin in one particular respect: 'in socialist society trade remains the only possible mechanism for distribution of consumer goods, and serves as a link between production and consumption. It helps to reveal the changing needs of society and to improve the planning of production of commodities required for their satisfaction' (p.712).

It does not of course follow from what we have said that there were not some in the '20s who appreciated that there was more to NEP than this, and that it indicated some modification in the view of socialism *per se* as a marketless and moneyless economy. Perhaps Bukharin in his later period held such a view (it was one of his disciples, Stetsky, who launched an attack on Kritsman's interpretation of War Communism). If so, such a view was hinted at obliquely and no more – implied rather than explicitly enunciated, still less advanced as a novelty and a challenge.

If I may be personal for a moment: when I wrote my *Russian*

Economic Development since the Revolution in 1927-28, I appended to the chapter on the transition to NEP what I find I called an 'Excursus on Money and Economic Accounting', which virtually interpreted and justified NEP as a system of monetary accounting resting on the market (which under socialist conditions would lack the chief defects it has under capitalism), – and with certain qualifications advocated the inclusion of an interest-charge in costs (on this question I seem to have been a little ambivalent). What I evidently had in mind was some kind of mechanism of the Lange-Lerner type (as it later came to be called by economists), and treated NEP as an expression of this. Subsequently, however, in the '30s, following the official line, I swung over to the justification of centralised planning as a mechanism of coordinated decision-taking, and criticised the Lange-Lerner type of mechanism as too decentralised and allowing too much play to market forces (which, indeed, I still think is true of the extreme form in which they proposed it).

CONTEMPORARY ISSUES

What bearing on these issues can subsequent experience in the '50s and '60s be said to have had, especially the mounting criticism of over-centralisation in the '50s and proposals in the '60s for various measures of decentralisation – the moves for so-called 'economic reform' in the Soviet Union and in other socialist countries? This represents important concrete experience of the working and of the problems of a socialist economy and of planning which certainly deserves to be sifted and its bearing on socialist theory (in particular traditional views about 'commodity production' under socialism) carefully analysed.

First there is the question of consumers' goods sold as commodities to individual consumers in the retail market to which we have seen that Stalin assigned a subordinate (as well as inconclusive) role. I feel no hesitation in saying that, if one is to have material incentives in production, this amount of freedom of choice in individual spending is a necessary corollary; and even if one did not have such incentives, I believe it is clear that consumers would be better off with (and would doubtless opt for) choice of spending in a retail market than with universal rationed issues in kind. (As for free issues and unconstrained choice, this implies a situation of general plenty which no socialist country shows any prospect of reaching within the foreseeable future).

But what about so-called producers' goods – supplies to industry of things as inputs, especially capital goods or investment goods? Why should not these at any rate be centrally allocated, without any intervention of market relations, and handled by means of what Stalin termed direct product exchange, even when agriculture is involved as well as industry? Here the actual experience to date of planned economies, as regards practicability and efficiency, must evidently afford the decisive criterion.

In this field there are a number of fairly clear conclusions to be drawn, which I myself as well as others have on occasion summarised. At the risk of boredom, let me try briefly to summarise these again, which I think can best be done under three main heads.

Firstly, it is practicable for planning to control directly (and if need be allocate) *some* things – 'key' products if you like – but by no means everything. The idea of *all* things being centrally controlled and coordinated turns out to be a romantic myth. This is partly a matter of planning time-table (there must obviously be an end-date, and if the experience, e.g. of last year's results, on which it builds, is not to be too obsolete, there must be a not-too-early starting-date as well), and partly of availability at the centre of reliable information (of which we shall speak further under another heading). Even at its most centralised in the early '50s Soviet planning has never dealt centrally with (in the sense, e.g., of setting planned output-targets for) more than 5000 products; while the balance method covered about 1,000 items. Yet the number of items in the official industrial nomenclature list amounted in 1960 to 15,000, and it was calculated that all-told there were more than 40-50,000 separate enterprises of one kind or another. In a Czech context, referring to price-setting, Ota Šik once referred to over a million items as needing to be priced. Nor is it at all realistic to reply to this by claiming that the computer can solve all this and that this is the age of the computer. The computers used to date in compiling input-output tables have handled no more than a few hundred products (for the 1959 Soviet table 157 for 83 industrial branches). This implies a fairly high degree of aggregation into product *groups* (steel or coal or machine-tools or shoes), and when used, e.g., for purposes of the balance method inevitably implies a sizeable margin of error (since production-coefficients *within* the aggregated group can differ appreciably – not to mention for separate enterprises).

It follows that quite a lot of decisions (numerically large if not proportionately so as well) will *have* to be taken of necessity at lower levels – preferably at the level of the industrial enterprise, since there the details of the production situation are best known as well probably as the demand for various products (so far as this is expressed in orders). If these lower-level decisions are not coordinated centrally (in any full sense at least), there seems no alternative to their being coordinated, to some extent and in some form, by the market or by market-indices. If supplies of producers' goods are not centrally allocated on a rationing or quota system, then it follows that they must be distributed by free contracting between enterprises – a form of wholesale trade in industrial supplies such as Kosygin in '65, announcing the new economic reforms, indicated as the logical future consequence of the decentralisation measures proposed (a forecast which in the Soviet Union has only been fulfilled to a very limited extent, although it was a key feature of the Hungarian reform and of the Czech proposals of '68). Such decentralised contracting, in Kosygin's words, would involve 'direct ties between producing and consuming enterprises'.

Secondly, there is what one may call the 'information limit' – which is something that has both a quantitative and a qualitative aspect. In any full sense the information needed for setting production-targets and coordinating with them needed industrial supplies can only come from the level of the plant or enterprise, and has to be fed 'upwards' from the periphery to the centre, from the point of production to the higher planning level. In a changing situation much of such data about production-potential, new products and methods, must have the character of estimates and be approximate rather than precise (sometimes it may be little more than 'hunches' by men on the spot who have the 'feel' of the situation, *but feel* rather than *know* for certain). Even the most detailed questionnaires submitted by the centre may ask what turn out to be vague questions or even the wrong questions in the sense of failing to elicit something that is relevant to a correct decision. This is apart from obvious problems of handling and interpreting the data submitted to the planning centre. At what economists are apt to call the macro-level such deficiencies may well be of negligible importance; but the more detail is involved in central decision-making – detail concerning micro-relations – the more significant are such defects likely to be relatively to what is involved.

Probably more serious is the '*bias*' latent in all such information fed to the centre when it is known that obligatory tasks imposed upon the enterprise will be dependent upon (at least affected by) the information supplied. I once heard a Hungarian woman-statistician, conducting an industrial input-output enquiry, say: 'I think that the data I get back from plants and enterprises will be pretty reliable and objective because they will regard its purpose as purely academic.' What she meant, of course, was that since the enquiry did *not* come from a Ministry or planning body, nothing about future tasks or performance of the industries in question would be affected by the replies that were given. When a request for data *does* come from a Ministry or planning body, it is, surely, only human nature that the management of an enterprise should have an inclination to understate production possibilities or reserves and overstate its supply-needs, if only on the quite legitimate grounds that unless it submits a conservative estimate of these, its actual production-performance in the coming period will be hampered by supply-shortages. Of course, the planners, suspecting such a bias, may seek to compensate for it by upward adjustment of targets; but doing this can only be a matter of guess-work, not of precise estimating, and if overdone (as so often in the past) the resulting *over*tight planning can only disrupt things by causing damaging supply-shortages and late deliveries, as well possibly as the harmful effects of so-called *stormirovka* (spurts of activity to catch up with targets towards the end of the planning period). Moreover, its long-run effect is likely to be cumulatively to enhance the information-bias at the level of enterprises.

Thirdly, there is the crucial consideration (which occupied so much Soviet discussion in the late '50s), that if decision-taking is centralised the only way in which the results can be transmitted to the lower levels is in the form of quantitative 'targets' or orders; and the form these production-targets take (in particular the unit in which they are measured) tends to have a distorting effect on the production pattern (a distortion that experience seems to show can often exceed that associated with market indices, e.g. profitability). This, apart from the fact that excessive reliance on 'orders from above' for every detail deprived managers and others at the production-level of all initiative, reducing them to the role of obedient sergeant-majors. Examples of this distorting effect are now sufficiently familiar. If the target is expressed in weight, it naturally pays the factory or enterprise to turn out relatively few objects that are heavy rather than more in number but lighter, whether it be nails, bedsteads or candelabra (*vide* the much-quoted *Krokodil* cartoon of a procession of workers bearing aloft a single gigantic nail, and headed 'the factory fulfils its plan'). If in textile weaving the product is measured in length, it pays to weave narrow cloth of the very simplest pattern. If output be expressed in gross value (the simplest way incidentally of enumerating a varied output, since arrived at by multiplying a number of items by selling price), this encourages so-called 'material-intensive' types of product, i.e. products embodying much (or expensive) materials or components, like tools made only of expensive materials or children's clothing made only of expensive materials. A neat example is given by Ellman: schemes for optimising the distribution of freight on railways, drawn up by experts, have never been carried out since transport plans are always expressed in ton-kilometres! In a particular case this bias can of course be met by changing (so far as practicable) the dimension in question (e.g. from *gross* to *net* value as in the clothing industry in '59). But *some* degree of bias attaches to almost *any* physical index – which is why Liberman in the '60s emphasised the *khozraschot* principle of profitability as providing a 'synthetic index' that would surmount the bias of the purely quantity-of-output kind. Sometimes in the past attempts have been made to correct such distortions by multiplying the number of additional indices used in plan-targets, such as cost-reduction ones or employment-limits or stipulations about minimal output-assortment. But the effect of this, as we have seen, is not only to complicate the planners' task but may well lead to conflict between the various success-indicators stipulated in planning instructions. (For example, in Poland as late as 1960 as many as 50 'success indicators' were quite commonly in use, some of which conflicted with others, some being in fact ignored in favour of the ones that the management treat as worthy of serious attention and hence exerting the dominant influence.)

COMMODITY-PRODUCTION AND SOCIALISM

Recapitulation of what we have arrived at in this paper is perhaps scarcely necessary. The conclusions reached are probably not at all new to you – although I am not aware of ever having seen them stated explicitly in print. Let it suffice at any rate to say merely this. The traditional view, apparently, that commodity-production and socialism are incompatible, still held by many on the Left (or Ultra-Left) today, must evidently be abandoned. The presence of a retail market for consumers' goods is clearly needed, to afford consumers' choice, so long as there is wage-payment according to labour and the production of consumers' goods is insufficient to supply all needs. But experience has also shown that there is a place for market-relations in the supply of producers' goods internal to industry, both as regards contractual trading relations (instead of centralised direct allocation) between industries and industrial enterprises and as regards a considerable range of detailed decisions about output that are best decentralised to the enterprise level (these latter being governed by market decisions in the shape of *khozraschot* or balance-sheet considerations, costs and prices, credit-facilities and the like). Exactly where the line is to be drawn between centralised decision and decentralised, although partly a question of principle, is, I believe, in large degree a matter of experimentation.

It follows that the economic relations characteristic of the first eight months of the revolution and of NEP, especially as regards industry, were *not* just due to Russia's economic backwardness and the preponderant position and influence of the peasantry. The latter of course made the introduction of NEP the more necessary, especially after the abnormality and excesses of 'War Communism'. But NEP embodied at the same time elements essential to a socialist economy, at any rate in its first or lower stage: something which should have been recognised in the discussions of the '20s and after.

The period of the '30s, with its remarkable achievements and its (unacknowledged) 'retreat from NEP' embodied both a positive and a negative element. Its positive achievement was, of course, its development of planning and a planning system, superimposed upon and limiting the market. Its negative aspect was the *over*-centralisation of economic decision-taking by the second half of the decade and the undue whittling down of the freedom of the production-unit to take independent production-decisions and to have contractual relations with other units. As for the 'higher stage' of socialism, usually called 'communism', the position is of course different. But an increasing proportion of human wants *will* then be supplied through social services in some form rather than through the market (what precisely the reaction of this will be upon inter-industrial relations and decision-making I believe it is impossible at this stage of history to say). But the situation will then be different, be it noted, *not* by virtue of some political campaign or 'cultural revolution' acting on the subjective factor of human motives, but by reason of objective economic development: namely that social productive powers have reached a sufficiently high stage of development to banish scarcity and to achieve plenty.

NOTES

1. Laszlo Szamuely, *First Models of the Socialist Economic System. Principles and Theories.* Akademiai Kiado, Budapest, 1974.